James McCosh

Locke's Theory of Knowledge

With a notice of Berkeley

James McCosh

Locke's Theory of Knowledge
With a notice of Berkeley

ISBN/EAN: 9783337219260

Printed in Europe, USA, Canada, Australia, Japan

Cover: Foto ©Thomas Meinert / pixelio.de

More available books at **www.hansebooks.com**

LOCKE'S THEORY OF KNOWLEDGE

WITH A NOTICE OF

BERKELEY

BY

JAMES McCOSH, D.D., LL.D., D.L.

PRESIDENT OF PRINCETON COLLEGE

AUTHOR OF "METHOD OF DIVINE GOVERNMENT," "INTUITIONS,"
"LAWS OF DISCURSIVE THOUGHT," "EMOTIONS," ETC.

NEW YORK

CHARLES SCRIBNER'S SONS

1884

TROW'S
PRINTING AND BOOKBINDING COMPANY,
NEW YORK.

TABLE OF CONTENTS.

DIVERS ASPECTS OF FIRST PRINCIPLES.

GENERAL INTRODUCTION.

THE aim of this Part of the Philosophic Series is to treat historically the chief topics which have been discussed dialectically in the previous Numbers. The special doctrine to be thus illustrated is that of first principles. The discussion on this subject began with Locke's denial of Innate Ideas in the First Book of his Essay on Human Understanding, published in 1690, and has been continued ever since, particularly by such original writers as Hume, Kant, and Herbert Spencer. Our work would be incomplete without a historical and critical review of these leaders of thought. All of them have exposed prevailing errors, and all of them have caught glimpses of important truth ; I have to add that all of them have promulgated serious error. Can we by any magnetic process draw out the pure metal and allow the dross to sink ?

Our notices will be critical as well as historical. But in criticism there are always principles involved, and these ought always to be formally stated, that all may perceive the ground proceeded on, and be able to sit in judgment on the critic. This I propose to do in this Introductory Section.

Believing as I do in first truths, I am convinced that

there has been confusion in the account given of them, and
consequent errors in the conclusions drawn. Much clearness may be imparted by attending to certain distinctions
which I would thus illustrate. If we are considering the
subject of gravitation, we may look first at it in its actual
operations as seen by the senses, say, in a body falling to
the ground; secondly, as a deep law in the very nature of
bodies; and thirdly, the expression of that law by Newton. We may in like manner, in inquiring into a fundamental law of the human mind, regard first its actual
operations falling under the eye of consciousness, say,
when on noticing an effect we look for a cause; secondly,
the law in the mind which is followed; and thirdly, the
axiomatic form taken by that law, that everything which
begins to be has a cause. The errors committed by the
defenders of primary principles have almost all arisen
from overlooking this threefold distinction. There is a
fourth principle which needs to be brought into prominence in the present day, when it is so much overlooked,
namely, that all intuitions look at things, and that this
should be expressed in the form which the generalized law
takes.

I. Our intuitions appear as PERCEPTIONS. We perceive
self in a certain state. We perceive external objects as
affecting us and resisting our energy. We perceive relations between things as that this quality implies a substance—say, this weight implies a heavy body; that this
effect, say a house on fire, implies a cause; and that
this thing A, being equal to B, which is equal to a third
thing, C, is also equal to C. We have also moral perceptions, as that this deceitful act is wrong and deserves
punishment. Under this aspect our primary truths are
before the eye of consciousness. Locke is right, so far as
these are concerned, in denying that they are innate; they

e forth only when the mind begins to act. Primitively they are all singular. There is a subsequent process involved in drawing the general law out of them.

II. Underneath these perceptions are REGULATIVE PRINCIPLES. These are not before the consciousness any more than the law of gravitation is before the senses. The bodily eye sees an apple fall to the ground, but does not see the law of universal gravitation which all the while is acting. Just as little does the internal eye see directly the fundamental laws of thought or belief. They are in the mind and deeply seated there, just as the power of gravitation is seated in matter. They constrain us to believe in our personal identity; that it is impossible for the boy to eat his apple and yet have his apple preserved to him; that every occurrence has a cause, and that hypocrisy is to be condemned. These principles may be said to be innate (and Locke is wrong when he denies this), for they are in the mind when it begins to act. They are in our very nature and constitution, and are often so appealed to by Bishop Butler and the Scottish School of Metaphysicians. On the supposition that there is a God who made us and gave us our endowments, they have the sanction of God and can plead his authority in behalf of their decisions. They are in our nature and founded on the Divine nature.

III. They may be generalized into PRIMITIVE LAWS OR AXIOMS. They are thus formed by a discursive process out of the primitive perceptions, just as the law of gravitation is formed by generalizing its individual operations. We perceive that we are the same person to-day that we were yesterday, and that we are the same to-day as we were a week ago, or a year ago, and thus reach the law, that we always carry with us an identity. We perceive that this effect has a cause, and that we would declare of every other effect that it has a cause, and thus lay down the rule that every effect has a cause.

Our primitive perceptions are varied and are innumerable. We have such perceptions every hour, I might almost say every minute, of our waking existence. We seem continually to have a consciousness of self and of body as affecting self, say, of the ground we stand on, of the chair we sit on, of the air we breathe. But as to the great body of them we are not at the trouble to form them into general laws. As being generated by regulative principles without our noticing them, we act according to them without being at the trouble to form them into laws; indeed, we do not so construct them except for certain purposes, only, in fact, for scientific, but especially for metaphysical ends. While constantly employed, they are not usually before the mind as laws, any more than the law of gravity is before the mind when we drop a hot body from our hand expecting that it will fall.

It is in the formation of these laws that error may come in. There is no error in our primitive regulating principles; they have the sanction of our constitution and of God. There will be no error even in our primitive perceptions so far as they are primitive, and unless we mix up prejudices with them. But there may be mistakes in the generalized axioms that we construct. There are apt to be mistakes because of the complication of the phenomena of the mind, and because we mix up derivative truths and reasonings of our own with the primary truths. It is from this cause that there are so many disputes in metaphysics, and whenever there are disputes there must be error, at least on one of the sides, perhaps in both. We make hasty generalizations, and then claim for them the authority of reason and of God. People say in their haste that every thing has a cause, and are led to draw back

only when they discover that this would compel them to
hold that God has a cause ; when, discovering that they
have committed a mistake, they put the maxim in a more
correct form, that every thing which begins to be has a
cause.   It is only by a very careful observation, along with
what Bacon calls " the necessary rejections and exclusions,"
that we are able from the singular and concrete operations
to enunciate precisely the general law which is the expression of the regulative principle.   But it is possible, by
exceedingly careful inspection, to get the general from
the singular, and to express it accurately, and when we do
so we have a genuine metaphysical philosophy.

I believe that by far the greater part of the confusion
and error on the subject of primary or fundamental truth
arises from overlooking these distinctions.   Those defending them make assertions, regarding them under one, which
hold true of them only under another aspect.   Those attacking them succeed in making a plausible statement only
by exposing them under one of these sides.   Descartes,
in standing so resolutely by them, contemplates them
mainly as faculties or powers lying deeply in the mind, in
short, as regulative principles.   " Lorsque je dis que quelque
idée est née avec nous, ou qu'elle est naturellement em-
preinte en nos âmes, je n'entends pas qu'elle se présente
toujours à notre pensée, car ainsi il n'y en aurait aucune ;
mais j'entends seulement que nous avons en nous-mêmes
la faculté de la produire." (*Trois objec.*, Rep. Obj. 10.)
Locke, in opposing them as ideas or perceptions in consciousness, succeeded in showing that these are not innate.   Kant, in calling them *a priori* principles, views them
as regulative principles in the mind.   Those who oppose
him show that the conscious perceptions are not *a priori* in
the mind.   In these historical papers I hope to show, as to
the authors criticised, what were the aspects they looked

at, and what those overlooked. In this way I hope on the one hand, to introduce clearness into a subject which has become so confused, and on the other hand, to give such an account of the constituent principles of the mind, as to remove the prejudices which have been entertained against them, and recommend them to candid minds.

Under the First of these Aspects they have been called Primitive Perceptions, Intuitions, Instincts, and Cognitions.

Under the Second Aspect they have been described as "native laws," "fundamental laws of thought," "forms." Plato (Rep., vii., 51) called it νοητὸς τόπος. Aristotle (De Anim., iii., 4), adopts the view but modifies it, saying it is right, provided it be limited to the noetic power and the forms be represented as not in readiness for action, but in capacity, not ἐντελέχεια, but δυνάμει.

Under the Third Aspect they have been called κοιναὶ ἔννοιαι, πρῶται ἔννοιαι, πρῶτα νοήματα, naturæ judicia, a priori notions, definitions, maxims, axioms.[1]

IV. Our intuitions or primitive perceptions LOOK AT THINGS. This is a point to be especially emphasized in the present day. It has been overlooked because of the almost universal prevalence of an erroneous metaphysical principle. It has been taken for granted commonly, without being positively asserted, that the mind can be cognizant, at least directly, only of itself. Locke, as we shall see, made it percipient only of its ideas, though he was apt to identify his ideas with things. Hume made all human knowledge consist of impressions and ideas without a mind to perceive or an object to be perceived. Kant, in answering Hume, started with assuming only presentations which he called phenomena, and labored from these to get real things, but without succeeding—as I believe

---

[1] See *Intuitions of the Mind*, P. I., b. ii., s. 2.

every one now acknowledges. The time has come for formally abandoning this philosophic heresy. We should assume that the mind knows things; not appearances, but things appearing. Appearances necessarily presuppose things appearing—even an image in a mirror implies a reflecting surface and rays reflected. In the very first exercise of our faculties we look at things: at the things perceived and the self perceiving them. It is a fact that we regard the colored surface before us, and the resisting energy in it, as realities. If we deny this we are virtually declaring that we cannot trust our cognitive powers, or rather that we have no cognitive powers, and we may give up, as Hume recommends, all philosophic inquiry and attend merely to our instinctive and acquired cravings, as we have no means of reaching positive truth.

It is a favorite mode of procedure in the present day to assume an hypothesis and then prove it to be true by showing that it accounts for every thing and puts it in the right place. The hypothesis that we know realities can stand this test; assume it, and we can go on consistently and find corroborations every hour, nay, every minute. But it is preposterous to make reality perceived a mere hypothesis; we know it quite as certainly as the hypothesis we put forward to explain it, or the supposed verifications. It is pleasant to have these, but they do not prove the known fact.

We are to assume that we know self and not self. Proceeding upon these we have other primitive perceptions. On comparing the present self with the past self at any given time, we know that we are the same. We know of this not-self that it exists independent of our cognition of it and exercises energy. As to many of our primitive perceptions, the object is not immediately before us. This is at once seen to be the case with the two perceptions last named. Thus, when I perceive that I am the same person to-day that I was yesterday, the self of yesterday is not before the consciousness. But it being brought before us by the memory we contemplate it, and then pronounce the judgment, which proceeds on the remembered fact. When we discover an effect, a thing effected, we decide that it must have had a thing causing it. This is the case with all our primitive perceptions of relations : we perceive them as in the things related.

In our moral perceptions the objects are not before us in the same sense as the self and not self are. But these perceptions all refer to things contemplated. It is upon an act of cruelty, believed to be a fact, that we pronounce the judgment that it is bad. It is in regard to a deed of self-sacrifice and benevolence that we declare it to be good. The act may not be before our senses, it may be far distant, or it may be long past, or it may be in the future, but it is upon the act supposed to have happened or to be about to happen, that the judgment is formed.

It is because this is the nature of our primitive perceptions that the first test of them is self-evidence. Since the days of Leibnitz, and especially since the time of Kant, the first and essential criterion of primitive truth has been commonly regarded as necessity, a necessity in our nature which leads us to know or decide in a particular manner that a quality implies a substance, that charity is good. But the proper statement is, not that an object is real and a proposition true because we are obliged to believe it, but we are obliged to believe it because we perceive the thing existing and the quality as being in the thing. The true mental process is that we look at the thing and perceive the quality in the thing; and we appreciate the benevolent action as in its very nature good.

SECTION I.

A BRIEF SKETCH OF LOCKE'S LIFE.[1]

John Locke was born at Wrington, in the pleasant fields of Somersetshire, August 29, 1632. His father was a lawyer possessed of moderate landed property, and took part in the great parliamentary and non-conformist upheaval. He exacted great respect from his son when a child, but when he grew up allowed him greater familiarity, a practice which the philosopher recommends. He got a place on the foundation of the famous Westminster school, and was there trained in the ordinary classical studies of the period. In 1651 he entered Christ Church, Oxford (in the grounds of which they still show the mulberry-tree which he planted), and there he was a diligent student and devoted himself specially to the branches requiring thought. He was reared amid the din of civil war. At school he must have heard the echoes raised by the execution of Charles I., and in college he was in the heart of the Royalist and Puritan contests. Like Bacon, two ages earlier at Cambridge, he did not derive much satisfaction from the studies pursued at college, and longed for new topics and a fresher mode of investigation. He did not follow any profession but he was particularly addicted to the study of medicine, in which Sydenham, the eminent physician of his day, declares that he acquired great

---

[1] See The Life of John Locke, by Lord King, 2 vols.; The Life of John Locke, by H. R. Fox Bourne, 2 vols.; Locke, by Thomas Fowler—the last giving a good sketch of his Life, but a meagre account of his philosophy.

knowledge and skill. He gave himself by turns to politics and philosophy, living mainly in Oxford and pursuing independent studies there. In 1664, during the Dutch war, he accompanied the king's envoy to the Elector of Brandenburg, and has left a graphic picture of his journey. In 1666, being called in to give medical advice, he became acquainted with Lord Ashley, afterward Lord Shaftesbury, and from that time became the medical adviser, counsellor, and friend of that tortuous statesman. Henceforth his life is partly in Oxford and partly with Shaftesbury, who appointed him to various offices. Though very prudent he became an object of suspicion to the Royal party, and Sunderland, by the king's command, ordered his expulsion. He was not expelled but deprived of his studentship by the dean and chapter of the college. He retreated from this strife to Holland, where he read and wrote and had close intercourse with a number of eminent men who met in each other's houses for discussion; with Le Clerc, Guenilon, the physician, with Limborch, and with the Remonstrant or Armenian party, to whom he attached himself rather than to the Calvinists. The Revolution of 1688 enabled him to return with Queen Mary to his own country, bringing with him the work which he had been pondering for years, the *Essay on Human Understanding*. Now in the maturity of his powers his literary activity was very great. He carried on an extensive correspondence, afterward published, on philosophic subjects with his admirer, William Molyneux, of Dublin, who introduced his essay into Dublin University, where it held sway down to the second quarter of this century, when it gave way before Kant. He carried on a keen controversy with Stillingfleet, Bishop of Worcester, who objected to his negative account of substance as undermining the doctrine of the Trinity. He wrote three letters on *Toleration*, on which his views, perhaps derived in part from John Owen, who was the Vice-Chancellor of Oxford when Locke was there, were very liberal for his day, though much behind those now entertained ; he would give no toleration to atheists or papists. In a constitution which he drew out for North Carolina he allowed hereditary slavery to exist. He wrote valuable papers on *Currency* and *Coin*. In 1695 he published *Essay on the Reasonableness of Christianity as delivered in the Scriptures*. He wrote a *Commentary* consisting of paraphrases and notes on the Epistles to the *Galatians, Corinthians, Romans*, and *Ephesians*, together with *An Essay for the Understanding of St. Paul's Epistles by consulting St. Paul himself.* All these are written in a reverent spirit, such as he always cherished toward God and Scripture, but are decidedly rationalistic.

His health had never been good, and latterly became worse. From 1691 he resided with Sir Francis and Lady Masham, the latter a daughter of Ralph Cudworth, the erudite defender of the older philosophy which Locke was now undermining. On October 27, 1704, he told Lady Masham that he never expected to rise again from bed. He thanked God he had passed a happy life, but now that he found all was vanity, and exhorted her to consider this world as a preparation for a better state hereafter. Next day he heard Lady Masham read the Psalms, apparently with great attention, until perceiving his end to draw near he stopped her and expired a few minutes after, in his seventy-third year.

We see what were the circumstances in which he was brought up. He lived when the Commons were limiting the authority of the crown ; when the Puritans were seeking to tear away every " rag of popery "; when the non-Conformists were rebelling against church authority, and the Arminians were softening the asperities of Calvinism. When he began to think for himself the ancient logic was still holding its place in the universities and the philosophy was largely analytic and deductive and couched in scholastic phrases. But a spirit was abroad fitted to break all this up as the returning sun does the ice in spring. The stars in the sky that presided over his birth were Bacon, Descartes, Herbert of Cherbury, Hobbes, and Gassendi. All these had declared more or less distinctly against Aristotle, who had ruled for so many centuries, and were introducing new methods of inquiry. Already Harvey, Boyle, and Newton were successfully prosecuting the observational method, and showing how rich mines of wealth it had opened. He was acquainted with the writings of all these men ; it is rather a curious circumstance that he seldom quotes them, but of all things he is resolute in preserving his independence and following a course of his own.

His characteristics among metaphysicians were his sagacity and independence, tempered with good sense. He was determined to look beyond appearances into the realities of things. Trained in an ancient university, but at a time when the old was passing away, educated for the bustling profession of medicine, mingling constantly with statesmen, with a social disposition and many attached friends, both in England and Holland, he had a large practical acquaintance with human nature and with mankind. He is bent above all things to have *determinate* (to use a phrase which he is anxious to introduce into philosophy) opinions of his own. It has to be added that having formed, by long observation and thought, a theory on a subject, he was apt to carry it too far and not notice the other truths by which it was limited. His was one of those greater minds which, unlike those which dwell only on differences, are disposed, as Bacon describes it, to fix their attention exclusively on resemblances to the neglect of exceptions and so form hasty generalizations.

If you look at Locke's portrait you have a good idea of his character. What strikes one at first is the prominence of the bones; brow, nose, cheek, and chin are all marked and decided. Our attention is at once fixed on these, and we do not notice the flesh or softer parts. It is a type of his mind with a strong and bony intellect, but without the finer emotions being visible, though they certainly existed like waters down in the fountain. His expression indicates thought, observation, profound sense, modesty, firmness, decision, and great independence of character. From the very look of him you would see that he is a man who thinks and acts for himself, who sets a high aim before him, whose honesty cannot be tampered with, and who cannot be either drawn or driven from his purpose.

You notice perhaps some irritability, and he tells us he was somewhat hasty in temper, but you perceive that it has been subdued by a stern judgment. In his little work on *The Conduct of the Understanding* he lays down some admirable rules for the guidance of the intellectual powers, but would lay too severe a restraint upon the affections —which are to be cherished and not eradicated. He was possessed of deep and genuine feeling, but it would have improved his philosophy had he given it as prominent a place as he did to the understanding. By looking more carefully at man's emotional and moral nature he might have been led to see that there are ideas of beauty and moral good which cannot be had from the only two inlets into the mind allowed by him, sensation and reflection. He was ever a man of independent thought and was in general a sincere lover of truth, but he was a little too self-dependent: he speaks rather too often and too strongly of his being actuated by a pure desire to discover truth. It might have been better perhaps, both for his philosophic and religious creed, if he had learned to distrust his judgment a little more, if he had realized that self-confidence is one of the sins to which humanity is liable, and allowed that the love of a favorite theory, such as that all our ideas come from sensation and reflection, may lead to the oversight of facts. Still, when we go along with him we feel that we are walking in a clear and bracing atmosphere with a man of high aim, of noble purpose, and vigorous step, and that to keep up with him is a healthy exercise fitted to invigorate the whole intellectual frame.

His style is described by Dugald Stewart. "It resembles that of a well-educated and well-informed man of the world rather than of a recluse student who had made an object of the art of composition. It everywhere abounds with colloquial expressions, which he had probably caught by the ear from those he had considered as models of good conversation, and hence, though it seems somewhat antiquated and not altogether suited to the dignity of the subject, it may be presumed to have contributed its share toward his great object of turning the thoughts of his contemporaries to logical and metaphysical inquiries" (*Dissertation*, Sec. I.). He can put wisdom in apt and apposite forms. "Good manners are the blossom of good sense, and it may be added of good feeling; for if the law of kindness be written on the heart it will lead to that disinterestedness in little as well as in great things, that desire to oblige and attention to the gratification of others which is the foundation of good manners." He has at times passages of literary beauty. "Thus the ideas as well as the children of our youth often die before us, and our minds represent to us those tombs which we are approaching, where, though the brass and the marble remain, yet the inscriptions are effaced by time and the imagery moulders away. The pictures drawn in our mind are laid in fading colors, and if not sometimes refreshed, vanish and disappear " (*Essay*, II., 19). He has a good deal of humor, the usual concomitant of good sense. On his way to Brandenburg, " I met lately accidentally a young sucking divine, who thought himself no small champion, who, as if he had been some knight-errant bound by oath to bid battle to all comers, first accosted me in courteous voice, but the customary salute being over I found myself assaulted most furiously, and heavy loads of arguments fell upon me. I, that expected no such thing, was fain to guard myself under the trusty broad shield of ignorance, and only now and then returned a blow by way of inquiry, and by this Parthian way of flying defended myself till passion and want of breath had made him weary, and so we came to an accommodation, though had he had lungs enough, and I no other use of my ears, the combat might have lasted as long as the wars of Troy." " One day when I rode out only to an airing I was had to a foddering of chopped hay or logic forsooth. Poor *materia prima* was canvassed cruelly, stripped of all the gay dress of her forms and shown naked to us, though I must confess I had not eyes enough to see her; however, the dispute was good sport and would have made a horse laugh, and truly I was like to have broke my bridle. The young monks (which one would not guess by their looks) are a subtle people, which dispute as eagerly for *materia prima* as if they were to make their dinner on it, and perhaps sometimes it is all their meal, for which others' charity is more to be blamed than their stomach. The professor of philosophy and moderator of the disputation was more acute at it than Father Hudibras; he was top full of distinctions, which he produced with so much gravity and applied with so good a grace, that ignorant I began to admire logic again, and could not have thought that 'simpliciter aut secundum quid materialiter et formaliter,' had been such gallant things which, with the sight of stroking his whiskers, the settling of his hood, and his stately walk made him seem to himself and me something more than Aristotle and Democritus. But he was so hotly charged by one of the seniors of the fraternity that I was afraid sometimes what it would produce, and feared there would be no other way to decide the controversy between them but by cuffs; but a subtle distinction divided the matter between them and so they parted good friends. The truth is hog-shearing is here much in its glory, and our disputing in Oxford comes as far short of it as the rhetoric of Carfax does that of Bilingsgate." I have given these extracts from his journal at such length because they furnish a more vivid picture, than I myself could have drawn, of the new philosophy represented by Locke, in its confidence and pride taking a parting look at the old philosophy, represented by the scholastic discussions, passing away in the midst of weakness and ridicule.

SECTION II.

SKETCH OF LOCKE'S GENERAL THEORY.

His theory is a simple one, some think scarcely equal to the complexity of nature. In his Epistle to the Reader he explains the occasion on which the thoughts arose in his mind. "Were it fit to trouble thee with the history of this essay, I should tell thee that five or six friends meeting at my chamber and discoursing on a subject very remote from this, found themselves very quickly at a stand by the difficulties that arose on every side. After we had a while puzzled ourselves without coming nearer a resolution of these doubts which perplexed us, it came into my thoughts that we took a wrong course; and that before we set ourselves upon inquiries of that nature it was necessary to examine our own abilities and see what objects our understanding were or were not fitted to deal with. This I proposed to the company, who all readily assented, and thereupon it was agreed that this should be our first inquiry."

His aim was to find what subjects the understanding was fitted to deal with, and for this purpose to discover how the mind gets its ideas and what is their nature. The work was written "by catches," and he acknowledges that intervals of "many long interruptions" caused "some repetitions."

His first position, to which he holds most determinedly, is that the mind has nothing innate. This he seeks to establish in Book I., arguing that man has no innate speculative principles, such as "that it is impossible for the same thing to be and not to be at the same time," that he has no innate practical or moral principles, and that the ideas supposed to be innate, such as that of God, are not so.

In Book II. he shows how we get our ideas. Locke is much addicted to speak of truths by means of images, and he supposes the mind to be, "as we say, white paper, void of all characters, without any ideas" (II. 1). He says that "external and internal sensation are the only passages that I can find of knowledge to the understanding. These alone, as far as I can discover, are the windows by which light is let into this dark room; for methinks the understanding is not much unlike a closet wholly shut out from light, with only some little opening left to let in external visible resemblances or ideas of things without; would the pictures coming into such a dark room but stay there and be so orderly as to be found

upon occasion, it would very much resemble the understanding of a man in reference to all objects of sight and
the ideas of them " (II.).

These two inlets he called Sensation and Reflection, or
external and internal sense. By these we get the materials of all our ideas. He defines idea as " the object of the
understanding when it thinks," and means by it much the
same as we would now describe as conscious states or
operations of the mind.

Upon these ideas are faculties operating. These are:

  I. Perception.   IV. Comparison.
  II. Retention.   V. Composition.
  III. Discernment. VI. Abstraction.

Briefly, the faculties (1) perceive; (2) retain; (3) distinguish between one thing and another; (4) compare, that
is, observe resemblances; (5) put objects in new shapes; (6)
separate a part from the whole. He shows how, from
these materials and by these faculties, we get all our ideas
simple and complex of the primary and secondary qualities
of matter, of space, power, substance, solidity, and infinity.

In Book III. he speaks of words in relation to ideas,
and makes some very important remarks, and some very
extravagant ones, as to the abuse of language. This subject does not come specially in our way. It is different
with Book IV., where he speaks of knowledge, opinion,
assent, and faith. Knowledge is represented as the perception of the agreement or repugnance of our ideas, not
of things, but with one another; in some cases the agreement being seen intuitively or directly, and in others by a
process in which there may be more or less certainty.

Locke's mind was filled with this theory, he kept it before him for twenty years, from 1670 to 1690, when he
published it; but he did not state it in a *determinate* way
(to use a phrase of his own), and did not notice other

truths which limited it. Catching the spirit of his times, he had an aversion to the scholastic nomenclature of the middle ages (he speaks with disdain of "their uncouth, affected, or unintelligible terms"), which continued to be used in philosophy down to the beginning of the seventeenth century. In his style he adopted the language of those who were reckoned as the models of talking and writing in his day. As a consequence his phraseology is often conversational and loose. This helped to gain him a hearing in his own age, but has led to his being misunderstood in later times. There have been many controversies as to his precise doctrine on certain points, as for instance, what power he gives to reflection as one of the inlets of knowledge, and what is the relation between his two inlets of ideas on the one hand, and the faculties represented as working upon these ideas on the other. I believe that on some points he has been misrepresented; he has been spoken of as an idealist, a sensationalist, and a rationalist. It will be necessary to examine these charges. I suspect that the *Essay on Human Understanding*, which used to be so famous, is not much read in the present day. The views of it which are entertained by students generally are commonly taken from histories of philosophy and compends, in which Locke is put into an artificial class, in which the comprehensiveness of his philosophy and his specialties are overlooked. It is necessary in these circumstances to have his system reviewed anew. This will enable us to determine exactly what was his view of the understanding, when it will appear that in some points he has been misunderstood both by his admirers and his opponents; that he has retained a larger portion of primitive truth than some give him credit for; while he has not retained enough to furnish a deeply settled foundation for truth.

SECTION III.

MEANING OF IDEA AND REFLECTION.

He defines "idea" as "the object of the understanding when it thinks," and uses it to express "whatever is meant by phantasm, notion, species." The schoolmen drew more or less clearly a distinction between these three phrases. By phantasm, a term derived from Aristotle, they designated the representation of a particular thing, say, of a lily. Notion was used only when some intellectual operation was employed in the formation of it, say, a general notion, or what is now designated concept. Species referred to visible appearance and to objects classified. Locke might have profitably looked to these distinctions; they would have saved him from much confusion; but he has an aversion to all scholastic distinctions. He seems to me to denote by it any of our conscious mental states, as we would now express it, all our sense perceptions, our recollections, our judgments, our moral approbations. As he employs it, the literal meaning of the word as an image always attaches to it, hence he has a difficulty in understanding what a general notion is; for when he regards it as an idea, he looks upon it not as a combination of things by points of resemblance, which it is, but as a figure or fancy which is inadequate to represent a class or concept.

It is evident that Locke views the mind as looking to ideas in all its exercises rather than to things. It will be necessary, as we proceed, to inquire how he gets from ideas to things. At this point Berkeley drove him to idealism, maintaining that there is no proof of anything but the idea; and Hume to skepticism, arguing that there is no reality in the idea. But it is certain that Locke thought he could, from the ideas, get to things. He identifies the ideas with the things they represent, and regards the understanding in looking at ideas as looking at real things. He tells us expressly, indeed, that "the mind knows not things immediately, but only by the intervention of the ideas it has of them" (IV., 4). But there are passages in which he speaks of the understanding as looking at material things. "To discover the nature of our ideas the better and to discourse of them intelligently, it will be convenient to distinguish them as they are ideas or perceptions in our minds, and [what seems an extraordinary statement from him] as they are modifications of matter in the bodies that cause such perceptions in us" (II., 8). But our present inquiry is about the meaning of the word. The subject of the relation of ideas to realities will require to be taken up in a later part of this paper.

But this may be the most suitable place for mentioning that I regard Locke as entirely successful in showing that the mind has not within it at its birth the ideas of which he speaks; that it has not images, phantasms, or abstract notions of any kind. In all this he has dissipated and scattered a whole cloud of errors which had for ages brooded over and darkened the whole subject of the origin and nature of ideas and knowledge.

There has also been a controversy about the use of the word reflection. The phrase was used by Gassendi, by whom it is supposed Locke was considerably influenced, to signify a faculty above sensation reviewing all the operations of the mind. Locke makes it, our observation "employed about the internal operations of our mind perceived and reflected on by ourselves" (II., 1). It denotes something more than we now express by the phrase self-consciousness, which signifies the knowledge of self in its present state. According to Locke it implies attention, which is an act of the will and is continuous. He says that the ideas of reflection "need attention." He denotes by it the act of the mind in voluntarily bending back and looking in upon its operations. When it was objected to Locke that he could not get our higher ideas, such as those of moral good, from his two inlets, it was answered by some, such as Leibnitz and Stewart, that he could get them from reflection. But this is entirely inconsistent with Locke's theory, which represents reflection as the eye looking in upon the operations of the mind, in which exercise it can see only what is in the mind, and therefore cannot see moral good unless it be already there; and this must be by some other power producing it.

SECTION IV.

OFFICES DISCHARGED BY THE FACULTIES.

What is the relation of the faculties to the two original inlets of knowledge? This is a subject on which Locke has not expressed himself very clearly. From his metaphorical expressions it looks as if ideas came into the mind from without. We can understand how this might be so far as sensible objects are concerned. When it is asked "how bodies produce ideas in us," it is answered, "that it is manifestly by *impulse*, the only way which we can conceive bodies operate in" (II., 8). But what does impulse mean when applied to an action on mind by matter? Then, it is not conceivable that our ideas by reflection, which are wholly within the mind, could have come from without.

He represents the ideas coming in by these inlets as *passive*, and such as the mind cannot get rid of. But it does not seem as if formed ideas come in after this manner, but merely the *materials* of ideas. Both the phrases *inlet* and *materials* are metaphorical and somewhat materialistic. It does not appear that the inlets furnish ideas till the faculties, till at least perception works upon them. " To ask at what time a man has first any ideas, is to ask when he begins to perceive ; having ideas, and perception, being the same thing " (II., 9). " Simple ideas are suggested and furnished to the mind only by those two ways above mentioned, viz., sensation and reflection " (II., 2). And yet a little further on he says, " Perception is the first faculty of the mind employed about our ideas " (II., 9) ; as if we had first ideas and then perceive them. " Our ideas being nothing but actual perceptions in the mind which cease to be anything when there is no perception of them " (II., 10). He says, " Perception being the first step and degree toward knowledge, and the inlet of all the materials of it ;" and again, " Perception is the first operation of all our intellectual faculties, and the inlet of all knowledge into our minds " (II., 9). How are we to bring a consistent whole out of these various statements, giving its office to sensation and reflection on the one hand, and to perception on the other ? Before we can answer the question we must notice that all the other faculties are employed about the ideas as well as perception. Thus he tells us that there is " no knowledge without discerning," that is, " distinguishing between the several ideas we have." In particular, he is obliged to give a large place to the faculties in discovering relations, such as those of identity, and of cause and effect.

Locke speaks everywhere of the ideas and knowledge which men may obtain " by the use and due application of their natural faculties" (I., 3). He asserts that "men, barely by the use of their natural faculties, may attain to all the knowledge they have without the help of any innate impressions, and may arrive at certainty without any such original notions or principles" (I., 3). Here we may notice his opposition to everything inborn, but at the same time his distinct recognition of the important offices discharged by the faculties. It looks as if, while denying innate ideas, he made the faculties perform somewhat of the same offices as the *a priori* principles, or primary truths, are supposed to do by their advocates. Had Locke carefully and systematically unfolded all that is in the faculties, it might have been seen that there is not after all so great a difference between his views and those of the philosophers who oppose him, as is commonly imagined. But it would thereby appear only the more clearly that he was guilty of a great and inexcusable oversight in not telling us precisely how much the faculties can do. The following passage helps to let us see what his views were: "Had they examined the ways whereby men come to the knowledge of many universal truths, they would have found them to result in the minds of men from the being of things themselves, when duly considered, and that they were discovered by the application of those faculties that were fitted by nature to receive and judge of them when duly employed about them" (I., 4). Here we have two very important principles. One is that knowledge comes from the *consideration*—he should have said from the *perception*—of the being of things; a most important truth, which will require to be separately considered. The other is that men obtain them by "the application of their faculties."

He certainly ascribes to the faculties very important functions. He gives them the power of *suggesting*, a capacity which might open up wide fields. Existence is an idea suggested to the understanding by every object (II., 7). Among all the ideas we have, as there is none suggested, so there is none more simple than that of unity (II., 16).

He allots a very important place to intuition. "Our highest degree of knowledge is intuitive without reasoning." "For if we will reflect on our own ways of thinking, we shall find that sometimes the mind perceives the agreement or disagreement of two ideas immediately by themselves without the intervention of any others; and this, I think, may be called intuitive knowledge. For in this the mind is at no pains of proving or examining, but perceives the truth as the eye doth light, only by being directed toward it" (IV., 2). "Some of the ideas that are in the mind are so there, that they can be by themselves immediately compared one with another, and in these the mind is able to perceive that they agree or disagree as clearly as that it has them. Thus the mind perceives that the arch of a circle is less than the whole circle" (IV., 17). He tells us "we have an intuitive knowledge of our own existence" (IV., 3). He goes so far as to declare, "It is on intuition that depends all the certainty and evidence of all our knowledge" (IV., 2).

Upon this intuitive knowledge demonstration proceeds, and in it "the mind perceives the agreement or disagreement of any ideas, but not immediately;" it is by intervening proofs in which each step has intuitive evidence. He maintains that of "real existence we have an intuitive knowledge of our own, demonstrative of God's, sensitive of some few other things. All this sounds very much like the doctrine of those who hold by *a priori* truth. I am pleased to find that he regards self-evidence—and not necessity, which Leibnitz and Kant do—as the test of intuitive truth. " Whether they come in view of the mind earlier or later, this is true of them, that they are all known by their native evidence, are wholly independent, receive no light, nor are capable of any proof one from another." But there is a fundamental error in his view of intuition. He cannot, in consistency with his general theory of the mind, looking only at ideas, make intuition look at things. All intuitions are judgments and involve a comparison of ideas.   This error was seen at an early date (1697) by King, author of the *Origin of Evil*, and at a later day by Reid, who remarks : " I say a sensation exists, and I think I understand clearly what I mean.   But you want to make the thing clearer, and for that end tell me that there is an agreement between the idea of that sensation and the idea of existence.   To speak freely this conveys to me no light, but darkness." [1]   The primary exercise of intuition seems to be an immediate perception of things without us and within us.   It is only thus we can construct a philosophic realism such as Locke meant to hold.

He gives a high and deep place to reason.   In replying to Stillingfleet he is able to say, " Reason, as standing for true and clear principles, and also as standing for true, and clear, and fair deductions from these principles, I have not wholly omitted, as is manifest from what I have said of self-evident propositions, intuitive knowledge, and demonstration."   He might have stated more strongly that he often appeals to reason ; and he was claimed by the Unitarians of last century as a rationalist both in philosophy and religion.   From the passage last quoted we discover what he means by reason and what offices he allots it ; it includes " true and clear principles," and also deductions from them.   It is especially important to notice that it em-

---

[1] See *Intuitions of the Mind*, Part I., Book ii.

braces "self-evident propositions, intuitive knowledge and demonstration." What is this but "the reason in the first degree" of Reid, "the fundamental laws of belief" of Stewart, and the "pure reason" of Kant? Again we discover that Locke meant to stand up for the deep and radical principles which the Scottish and German schools have been defending and settling. But while he means to do this I am not sure that he has done it. For at what place in his system does reason come in? It is certainly not among the inlets of ideas and knowledge, and it does not appear in the list of the faculties working on the ideas. But he certainly brings it in, consistently or inconsistently, and I can only suppose that he makes it an exercise, probably a sort of combined exercise of the faculties. This only makes us regret the more that he has not unfolded more fully the powers embraced in these faculties as they look at things. Had he done so he might have found that these faculties and their properties are truly innate, though the ideas which they produce cannot be said to be so.

SECTION V.

HOW THE HIGHER IDEAS OF THE MIND ARE FORMED.

Having set aside all innate ideas in Book First of his Essay, Locke proceeds, in Book Second, to show how ideas are actually formed: this is from the two sources Sensation and Reflection, and by the Faculties working on the materials thus supplied. He shows this specially as to the ideas which are farthest removed from sense, and are supposed to be innate. It may serve a good purpose to look at the way in which he fashions some of the deepest and highest ideas which the mind of man can form. The charge against him is that he cannot form them by the means he calls in.

Existence is "an idea suggested to the understanding by every object" (II., 7). The correct account is that we know objects as existing, and do not need a suggestion. *Unity* is also represented as a suggested idea, whereas it is involved in the perception of things which are known first as singular. *Our own existence* is known intuitively. This is all right, but surely this implies a knowledge not through ideas but directly. At this place we see clearly the unsatisfactory nature of the theory of knowledge only through ideas.

Body.—It is difficult to determine how Locke makes us reach the knowledge of body. He tells us expressly " 'tis evident the mind knows not things immediately, but only by the idea it has of them " (IV., 3). But he has not succeeded in showing how from an idea supposed to be in the mind he can reach by any legitimate process an object external to the mind and extended. This, however, will require to be separately considered. He distinguishes primary and secondary qualities (II., 8). The Primary "are utterly inseparable from matter, in whatever state it be." How he knows that primary qualities are inseparable from matter he does not tell us. He says that "the ideas of primary qualities of bodies are *resemblances* of them," as if the idea of gold could be properly described as having a resemblance to gold. There is, certainly, some correspondence, though resemblance does not seem the exact word; but how can he know this when he does not perceive the bodies? "The ideas produced in us by the secondary qualities have no resemblance of them." I believe that there is a distinction between the primary and secondary qualities of bodies. But I am not sure that it has been accurately drawn by Locke. Primary qualities resolved by Locke, very properly, into extension, solidity, and motion, are perceived at once, whereas secondary qualities, such as heat, are mere organic affections for which we argue a cause, and science finds it in molecular motion.

Space.—He is in the same difficulty here as in regard to body, of getting it from an idea in the mind which has no spatial properties. He very properly says that our idea of space is got from touch and sight; I believe he might have said that we get it from all the senses, as by all the senses we know our bodies as extended and resisting our energy.

Time.—It is evident that he cannot get this idea from sensation, so he gets it from reflection: by reflecting on the succession of our ideas. At this point the defect of his theory has been pointed out by Leibnitz and Cousin. Reflection can perceive only what is in the mind, and cannot perceive succession unless it be already there. Time is one of those ideas which come in always in the concrete with the exercise of the faculties; in memory we recall an event as having happened in the past.

Substance.—Evidently he is greatly troubled with this idea, and yet he has not the courage to avow it. Stillingfleet, a man of scholarship, though not of much philosophical ability, charges him with denying or at least overlooking this idea. Locke wrote a courteous and elaborate reply in which he shows a good deal of fencing, but no very decisive statement. He is indignant at his opponent for making him deny the existence of substance. He argues that it exists, but certainly not on grounds very consistent with his theory. He acknowledges that substance is unknown to us (II., 23); he evidently cannot get it either from sensation or reflection, but he asserts, "all sensible qualities carry with them a supposition of a substratum to exist in" (II., 23). "We cannot conceive how sensible qualities should subsist alone, and therefore, we suppose them to exist in some common subject." Here he makes our conception a test of truth, and resorts to a supposition which he cannot justify on his theory. We know the substances mind and body as having being, independence of our observation of them, and as having potency.

Power.—His views on this subject, which has come into such prominence since the days of Hume, contain some important truths, but are very far from being adequate. Power being the source from which all action proceeds, the substances wherein these powers are when they exert this power are called causes (II., 21). I am glad to find him placing power in substance. His account should be quoted in full (II., 21): "The mind being every day informed by the senses of the alteration of those simple ideas it observes in things without, and taking no notice how one comes to an end and ceases to be, and another begins to exist which was not before; reflecting also on what passes within itself, and observing a constant change of its ideas, sometimes by the impression of outward objects on the senses, and sometimes by the determination of its own choice; and concluding from what it has so constantly observed to have been, that the like changes will be made for the future in the same things by like agents and by the like ways; considers in one thing the possibility of having any of its simple ideas changed, and in another the possibility of making that change, and so comes by that idea we call power." He *concludes*, but from what premises he does not tell us, and from this theory he cannot find a premise which will guarantee such a wide conclusion. He simply tells us, "the mind must collect a power somewhere able to make that change, as well as a possibility of the thing itself to receive it." The word *must* makes the appeal to necessity which he cannot legitimately employ. " Again, from the observation of the constant vicissitude of things we get our ideas of cause and effect " (II., 37), a theory which enables Hume to draw all his skeptical conclusions, that we have no idea of cause beyond that of observed antecedence, and no evidence that cause operates beyond our experience. I believe that he is right in drawing our idea of cause from both sensation and reflection, but "that the mind receives its idea of active power clearer from reflection on its own operations than it does from any external sensation." He has some very positive ideas as to the extent and limits of power which he cannot draw from his inlets and capacities. "It is as impossible to conceive that ever bare incogitable matter should produce a thinking, intelligible being, as that nothing should produce something."

This may all be good reasoning, but Locke has nothing on which to found it.

Infinity.—He denies that he has a positive idea of infinity (II., 17). Yet he stands up for its existence. " Man knows that nothing cannot produce a being, therefore there must be something eternal " (IV., 10). The conclusion is right, but he does not prove it. He assures us, on what evidence he does not say, "Wherever the mind places space itself by any thought, either amongst or remote from all bodies, it can in this uniform idea of space nowhere find any bounds, any end ; and so must necessarily conclude, it by the very nature and idea of each part of it to be actually infinite " (II., 17). He has some fine glimpses of the truth which we will speak of when we come to consider the idea of God.

Moral Good.—At this point Locke's oversights were first seen in England, which has always been jealous of every thing seeming to bear against morality. These were pointed out by the third Lord Shaftesbury, the grandson of his friend and patron. Certainly the philosopher's views on this subject are lamentably meagre. He does not get the idea of moral good from reflection; indeed he could not do so according to his theory, as reflection only sees what is already in the mind. He derives it openly and avowedly from sensation. "Things are good or evil only in reference to pleasure or pain; that we call good which is apt to cause or increase pleasure" (II., 20). He makes good not to be a thing in itself, but merely a relation. "Moral good and evil is only the conformity or disagreement of our voluntary actions to some law whereby good and evil is drawn on us from the lawgiver; which good and evil, pleasure and pain attending our observance or breach of the law by the decree of the lawgiver, is that we call reward and punishment" (II., 28). In this he makes morality depend on an arbitrary appointment on a law for which he can-bring no defence, and a God whose ways he cannot justify. The moral evil is bad, not in itself, but because there is punishment attached. Whereas, the true statement is that punishment is attached to it because it is evil. Yet he thinks he is able by this unsatisfactory genesis to reach "a natural law," "discoverable by our natural faculties." He reaches the conclusion, "The idea of a Supreme Being infinite in power, goodness, and wisdom, whose workmanship we are, and on whom we depend; and the idea of ourselves as understanding rational beings, being such as are clear to us, would, I suppose, if only considered and pursued, afford such foundations of our duty and rules of action as might place morality among the sciences capable of demonstration; wherein I doubt not but from self-evident propositions, by necessary consequences as 'incontestable as those in mathematics, the measures of right and wrong might be made out to any one that will apply with the same indifferency and atten-

tion to the one as he does to the other of these sciences"
(IV., 3). The language here employed leads me to consider—

The Idea of Necessity.—He is often appealing to a necessity. He speaks of certain and universal knowledge as having "necessary connection," "necessary coexistence,"
"necessary dependence" (IV., 3). We are able to see how
he could reach demonstration, all the propositions in which
are seen to be true intuitively; the question is, Could he
do it consistently? "In some of our ideas there are certain
relations, habitudes and connections, so visibly included in
the nature of the ideas themselves, that we cannot conceive
them separable from them by any power whatsoever. And
in these only we are capable of certain and universal knowledge. Thus the idea of a right-angled triangle necessarily
carries within it an equality of its angles to two right
angles" (IV. 3). He thinks he has like principles in ethics,
and so thinks they are capable of demonstration. All this
is apparently after the method of the rational school, and
it is not easy to see how he could draw it from his experiential principles. Again we are led to regret that he
has not determined for us what is in this reason, with its
"certain relations, habitudes and connections." We have
yet to consider as illustrating these points—

The Idea of God.—He tells us how we come by this
idea: "I think it unavoidable for every considering,
rational creature that will but examine his own or any
other existence to have the notion of an eternal being who
had no beginning" (II., 14). He refers his proof to the
faculties. "We are capable of knowing certainly that
there is a God, though God has given us no innate ideas
of himself, though he has stamped no original characters
on our minds wherein we may read his being; yet having
furnished us with those faculties our minds are endowed

with, he hath not left himself without a witness, since we
have sense, perception, and reason, and cannot want a clear
proof of him as long as we carry ourselves about us"
(IV., 10). He thinks he can reach in this way : " The
eternity of that infinite being which must necessarily have
always existed " (II., 114). By a like exercise of the faculties he clothes the Divine Being with his other perfections.

What was needed in Locke's day, what is still needed,
is an inductive exposition of all that is comprehended in
these faculties, in the intuition and the reason to which
Locke is so constantly employing. This was what was at-
tempted by Reid and Kant ; but the attempt has to be
renewed to reduce the systems to a consistent whole and
above all to make them thoroughly conform to the principles of the mind.

SECTION VI.

WAS LOCKE AN IDEALIST ?

Certainly no one uses the word "idea" so frequently.
I believe that Berkeley drove his theory logically to idealism, yet Locke was undoubtedly a determined realist, believing in the existence of a mind as well as of ideas, and
of a body as well as a mind.

He defines idea, "Whatsoever is the object of the understanding when it thinks " (I., 1). It would have been
more correct to say that idea is the state of the mind when
it thinks of an object. His view is repeated in the fuller
definition, "Whatsoever the mind perceives in itself, or is
the immediate object of perception, thought, or understanding, that I call an idea " (II., 8). This seems to me
clearly to make the object of which a man thinks to be
within the mind. The difficulty in which Locke, and all

metaphysicians who agree with him in making the mind percipient only of things within itself, here faces us : how from an idea in the mind can we get something out of the mind by any logical or legitimate process ? Already idealism has got an entrance and great difficulty has been experienced in expelling it. It takes its full form and assumes its full significance in the definition of knowledge in Book Fourth, " <u>Since the mind in all its thoughts and reasoning hath no other immediate object but its own ideas, which it alone does and can contemplate, it is evident that our knowledge is only conversant about them</u> " (IV., 1). So he goes on to define knowledge " to be nothing but the perception of the connection and agreement and repugnancy of any of our ideas. In this alone it consists." The common definition of knowledge is the agreement of our ideas with things. But in Locke's account things are left out, and it is difficult to discover how he finds things, or at least things external to the mind. I see no way in which he can logically extricate himself from idealism, which believes only in what is in the mind.

But Locke's good sense made him a very decided realist, in spite of his theory. He has a way in which he reaches a reality out of the mind. "The power to produce any idea in our mind I call quality of the subject wherein that power is. Thus a snow-ball having the power to produce in us the ideas of white, cold, and round, the power to produce those ideas in us as they are in the snow-ball I call qualities ; " and then he speaks of primary and secondary qualities (II., 8). But by what logical process can he reach those qualities in body, say of hot, cold, and round ? Those qualities, say that of roundness, are not in the idea which is not round. An idea without roundness could never give a notion, much less a knowledge, of roundness ; any argument to this effect would be a paralogism

and have more in the conclusion than in the premises.
It is clear that Locke is left without any means of consistently reaching roundness, or any other external quality
involving extension. The pronounced realist is thus driven
by his theory into idealism.

But error, like vice, leads to evil consequences, which
may in the end be made the means of correcting it.
Logic is as inflexible a disciplinarian as morality. Berkeley, as we shall see, carried out Locke's theory as to ideas
to its legitimate conclusion. If we have no direct perception or knowledge of external things, but only of ideas, it
was argued, then we can have no proof of the existence of
anything but these ideas ; even if there be such gross corporeal things as atoms, molecules, and masses they could
not possibly be known by us. There is no need of sup-
posing, certainly not of believing, that there are any such
gross bodies really existing; every end supposed to be
produced by them may be accomplished by the ideas.
There is left us a grand ideal world, created by God, and
forever in the vision of God, who hath given us the power
of contemplating it, and so operating upon it as to gather
experience, and to act upon it.

This is a beautiful speculation, but it is not consistent
with consciousness, which shows us as knowing external
objects. As the theory violated our natural convictions,
it was necessary that the avenger should come, and he
appeared in the *Treatise of Human Nature*, by David
Hume (1739). Proceeding on the principle of Locke,
carried out by Berkeley, that we do not know things, he
showed that we have only impressions, and ideas, the repro-
ductions of them, the latter being fainter than the former.

It was at this point that the Scottish school, with
Thomas Reid as the founder, and Dugald Stewart and
William Hamilton as its most distinguished disciples, met

the skeptic. Reid tells us that he was carried along by
the doctrine till he saw what consequences it produced in
the philosophy of Hume, when he was led to draw back
and review the whole ideal theory. Reid's own theory was
hesitating and uncertain. He talked of sensation *suggesting* a perception, thereby cumbering his doctrine of immediate sense perception. Hamilton corrected this vacil-
lating doctrine by making sense perception direct, but
then he unfortunately made all our knowledge relative
and not positive. The inquiry needs to be taken up at
this point and prosecuted anew.

SECTION VII.

WAS LOCKE A SENSATIONALIST ?

Locke's Essay was translated into French at the beginning
of the eighteenth century, but was not much known till it
(with Newton's *Principia*) was strongly recommended by
Voltaire on returning from his visit to England. The
French accepted only one half of the philosophy of the Eng-
lishman. The Abbé Condillac in his *Traité des Sensations*
labored to reduce the original inlets of knowledge to one,
and thus founded the sensational school which prevailed in
France down to the end of last century, greatly to the de-
basement of mind and morality. Taking their views from
French writers, rather than from Locke himself, the German metaphysicians from and after Leibnitz (who appre-
ciated while he opposed Locke) down to within the last
age spoke of Locke as a sensationalist, indeed as the repre-
sentative sensationalist. But Locke calls in two fountains of knowledge. His language is express: "The other
fountain from which experience furnisheth the understanding with ideas is *the perception of the operations of our own*

mind within, as it is employed about the ideas it has got, which operations, when the soul comes to reflect on and consider, do furnish the understanding with another set of ideas which could not be had from the things without, and such are perception, thinking, doubting, believing, reasoning, knowing, willing, and all the different actings of our own mind, which we being conscious of and observing in ourselves do from these receive into our understandings as distinct ideas as we do from the bodies affecting our senses. This source of ideas every man has solely in himself, and though it be not sense as having to do with external objects, yet it is very like it and might be properly called internal sense. But as I call the other sensation, I call this reflection" (II., 1). Condillac argued that as reflection had no innate idea and could not create anything of itself, and as everything in the mind previous to the exercise of reflection was got by the external sense, so all we have after can only be sensations, it may be transformed—they called them *transformes sensations ;* but Locke, whether logically or illogically, held that Reflection is a distinct inlet of ideas, higher than those of the bodily senses. The mind gets ideas from material things (how, he cannot very well show, as it does not perceive bodies directly) ; so it also gets a new kind of ideas from its own actings (this is more easily understood) as it observes them. "The mind furnishes the understanding with ideas of its own operations" (II., 1). Upon these, as we have seen (*supra*, Sec. IV.), he makes the Faculties to work, and thus gets, in a not very satisfactory manner (*supra*, Sec. V.), our higher ideas. Helvetius and the Encyclopedists multiplied *transformed sensations* till they got rid of God and Good ; so Locke and his English followers fashioned what we may call *transformed reflections* till they got a sort of rationalistic theology and utilitarian morals which prevailed for several ages. It thus appears that Locke was not a sensationalist, as he clearly and emphatically makes reflection a source of ideas, and is thus distinguished from Hobbes, from Condillac, the French Encylopedists and their whole school. British writers have always felt this.

SECTION VIII.

LOCKE WAS AN EXPERIENTIALIST.

While Locke was not a sensationalist, he was an experientialist—to adopt a phrase which has been conveniently coined since his day. It is his avowed doctrine, "Let us then suppose the mind to be, as we say, white paper, void of all characters, without any ideas; how comes it to be furnished? Whence has it all the materials of reason and knowledge? To this I answer in one word, from experience. In that all our knowledge is founded, and from that it ultimately derives itself. Our observation, employed either about external, sensible objects, or the internal operations of our minds, perceived and reflected on by ourselves, is that which supplies our understanding with all the materials of thinking" (II., 1). But the account is not free from ambiguity. Our observation brings us all our knowledge, but from two sources—sensation and reflection, and these are prior to observation. The manufacturer works all his own cloth, but he has to get wool to start with. Not only so, but he has to use machines to weave it. So it is with the understanding, according to Locke's own theory, when fully expanded. All is from observation, but it is the observation of something within and without, independent of our observation. Then it is by observing faculties, which have functions, and these are not the product of observation. Surely these might be called innate. So far

the maxim requires to be modified and explained. I believe this is what Leibnitz meant when, after allowing that
there was nothing in the intellect which was not previously
in the senses—always, in Locke's theory, including both
the external and internal senses—he adds, *nisi intellectus
ipse.*

There is an ambiguity, which has seldom or never been
noticed, in the use of the term experience. Sometimes it
means a mere individual experience, say the experience of
anticipating a cause when we fall in with an effect. In
this sense all intuitions, all *a priori* principles, fall within
our conscious experience. These individual experiences, it
is needless to show, do not constitute a science or a philosophy. But when from a number of individual experiences
we rise to a general law, this is a different thing, and this
is commonly called experience in speculative philosophy.
Locke never seems to have inquired what observations
were required to establish a general law. He does not
appear to have ever discovered that experiences, however
numerous, could not establish a universal law, which must
hold good beyond our experience. This subject has had
to be discussed since his day by the profound minds of
Hume, Kant, and J. S. Mill, and needs still to be cleared
up.

SECTION IX.

WAS LOCKE A RATIONALIST?

Locke's philosophy has certainly both a sense side and
an intellectual side ; both an experiential and a rational
element. The former was observed and accepted in France
in the last century, and was observed without being accepted in Germany. The latter was the more fondly con-

templated among English-speaking people, both in Great Britain and in the United States. In France his system was driven to sensationalism, and from the time of Kant almost to our day, he was called a sensationalist in Germany. But a very cursory reading of his works shows that Locke was utterly opposed to sensationalism, so far, at least, as it tended to sensualism. His English readers saw this all along.

In religion his spirit and tendency were rationalistic. In his Bible Commentaries, and in all his writings, he treats the Scriptures with profound reverence; but he is not partial to those doctrines which do not commend themselves to human reason. He recognizes the distinction drawn by Abelard and others between propositions contrary to reason and propositions above reason, and is willing to admit the latter when they clearly have the authority of God; but he is opposed to every kind of enthusiasm, extravagance, and mysticism. The Unitarians of last century, who denied the Deity of Christ and the Atonement, were fond of claiming his name and quoting his authority. In philosophic discussion he gives a deep place to intuition as the immediate perception of truth. He allots very important offices to the faculties. He is constantly appealing to reason, both as a discursive process, that is, reasoning, and as "the principle of common reason" (I., 4), and he regards mathematics as demonstrative, and would make ethics the same. During the last age, while the German historians of philosophy were calling him an empiric and a sensationalist, there were British writers who were showing how high the view which he presented of the human understanding, and what great truths he defended, such as Henry Rogers, in his *Essays;* Professor Bowen, in his *Philosophic Discussions;* and Professor Webb, in his *Intellectualism of Locke.*

`

SECTION X.

THE RELATION OF LOCKE'S THEORY TO THE VARIOUS ASPECTS OF FIRST TRUTHS.

In the opening of this paper I have called attention to three aspects of primitive or *a priori* principles. I mean to examine the chief modern philosophic systems in the light of these distinctions. It is evident that Locke did not observe the difference between the three aspects.

I. He regards innate ideas mainly as perceptions in consciousness. The original meaning of the word, that is, an image, likeness, or phantasm, always adheres to it in his apprehension. " Ideas being nothing but actual perceptions in the mind, which cease to be anything when there is no perception of them " (II., 10) ; " having ideas and perception being the same thing " (II., 1). Under this aspect he is right in declaring that they are not innate. They are not in the mind prior to birth or at birth. They rise up as the faculties are exercised. They constitute an individual experience. Not only so, but they cannot transcend the original inlets of knowledge—whatever these may be—certainly most of them may be traced to sensation and reflection as their fountains.

I think that Locke has been obliged to allow, that in the exercise of the faculties, ideas which I regard as new are generated. This being so, there may be perceptions, such as that of time and substance, not derivable directly from sensation and reflection. Now he is right in maintaining that none of these is innate. Herein his criticism is successful, and it has delivered philosophy from a whole host of imaginary entities in the shape of already formed ideas ready to come forth, on occasions presenting themselves, as writing by invisible ink is when a chemical process is applied to it.

II. The great omission of Locke is in overlooking primitive principles under the second aspect as regulative principles. It was in this light that they were viewed by Aristotle when he called νοῦς the τόπος ειδῶν not εν ἐντελέχεια but εν δυνάμει. This was the view taken by Descartes. "While I say that some idea is born with us, or that it is naturally imprinted on our souls, I do not understand that it presents itself always to our thought, for there is no thought it does so, but I understand that we have in ourselves the faculty to produce it. It was at this point that Locke was corrected by Leibnitz, when he added *nisi ipse intellectus;* maintaining that the intellect is innate though the actual ideas or perceptions are not, and that the innate principles" are in us before we perceive them (*Nouv.-Essais*, II., 1). Herein, too, Locke was improved by Kant, who places in the mind *a priori* principles, ready to be imposed on the objects of possible experience. Herein, too, Reid noticed the same truth, when he called in the principles of common sense, and Stewart, when he called them fundamental laws of belief. But whatever defects there may be in Locke's philosophy, he is ready to express the facts, whether they are reconcilable with his theory or not. His beliefs and his expressions are often sounder than his system. His honesty leads him to make statements which seem to be fatal to his favorite opinions. In answering Mr. Lowde, he says of supposed innate notions: "Before they are known there is nothing of them in the mind but a capacity to know them when the concurrence of those circumstances, which this ingenious author thinks necessary in order to the souls exerting them, brings them into our knowledge" (II., 28, *foot-note*).

III. We have seen that our intuitive perceptions may be generalized, when they become axioms or maxims. So far as they are not correctly drawn from the singular exercises they may be a source of error, widening like the darkness of an eclipse. It has to be added that from their subtle character, and from their being mixed up with other and empirical operations of the mind, there is very apt to be inaccuracies in the expression of them, breeding the confusion and controversies which are so apt to appear in metaphysics. But so far as they are correctly generalized they are as certain as our primitive perceptions, which are founded on the regulative principles of the mind, which have the sanction of our constitution and the authority of the God who gave us our constitution. How does Locke's philosophy stand toward them ?

"First, he is altogether right in saying that under this aspect primary truths are not innate. Locke is again successful here, and in consequence has carried with him on the general question multitudes who do not see that this is not the whole question, who do not see that there may be in the mind innate faculties with their laws, while there are no innate general axioms. Locke's favorite example in his First Book of a supposed innate principle is that " it is impossible for the same thing to be and not to be at the same time." He shows successfully that children and savages, in whom we might expect it if it is native, have no such conscious principle, and that they would not understand it if presented to them. " Such kind of general propositions are seldom mentioned in the huts of Indians, much less are they found in the thoughts of children or any impressions of them on the minds of naturals " (II., 3).

Secondly, he sees that these general propositions are derived from particular instances. " It is certain that not all, but only sagacious heads light at first on these observations and reduce them into general propositions, not innate, but collected from a preceding acquaintance and reflection on particular instances " (I., 2).

Thirdly, he does not see what they are generalizations of. They are not generalizations of external facts, like those of natural history or astronomy. They are generalizations of our primitive perceptions which grow out of the innate and constituent principles of the mind. On noticing a thing at a certain place we decide that it cannot be that this thing has passed out of existence, and we perceive that we would so decide in every like case, and generalizing our judgments, we declare that it is impossible for the same thing to be and not to be at the same time. This is not like the ordinary laws of nature discovered by induction, say the law of gravitation, which may or may not hold true in all worlds, but is true universally, and seen to be so by a necessity of thought.

Locke is further right when he says that these maxims do not furnish evidence of the particular instance. "The consideration of these axioms can add nothing to the evidence or certainty of its knowledge " (IV., 7). The truth is the evidence to us of the general depends on the particular, and not the evidence of the particular upon the general. "If one of these have need to be confirmed to him by the other, the general has more need to be let into his mind by the particular than the particular by the general. For in particulars our knowledge begins and so spreads itself by degrees to generals " (IV., 7). When I see the stick A of the same length as the stick B, which is again of the same length as the stick C, I judge and decide at once that A is of the same length as C, without getting any assurance from the axiom, that "things which are equal to the same thing are equal to one another."

Ile sees that the generalized maxims serve some good

purpose. "They are of use in the ordinary methods of teaching science as far as they are advanced." "They are of use in disputes for the silencing of obstinate wranglers and bringing those contests to some conclusion" (IV., 7). But why or how they should do so, unless they have authority? and whence their authority except from our nature and constitution, which are certainly innate? What is thus brought before us enables us to answer a plausible objection by Locke which has led some to discard innate principles. "Not only those few propositions which have had the credit of maxims are self-evident, but a great many, even almost an infinite number of other propositions are such," and he gives as examples that two and two are four, and that yellow is not blue. I am sure that the number of such propositions is almost infinite. They are pronounced upon our cognition of individual things. These propositions are all singular. But we are at the trouble to generalize only a few of them into maxims, such as the axioms of Euclid and of rational mechanics and generally metaphysical principles. Locke was tempted by his aversion to innate ideas of every kind to set too little value on these fundamental principles. Being put in the form of laws, which all science requires to be, they are the connecting links of many of the sciences, as for instance of the sciences of quantity, of energy, of logic—where we have the dictum of Aristotle, and of ethics, which assumes that wrong differs from right.

In this review I have sought so far as possible to enter into the very thoughts of the author, and this even when I do not agree with them. I have labored to look at things from his point of view before venturing to criticise him. In most of his tenets which have been controverted since his time I partly agree and partly disagree with him. As a truly honest inquirer he had commonly a large amount of truth in his doctrines; but I have been obliged to point out incorporated errors, commonly originating in his adherence to a favorite theory. Every one has noticed the apparent inconsistencies in his statements; I believe they arise from his discovering at times and acknowledging truths which cannot be reconciled with his general doctrine.

It is clear that he represents the mind as not directly perceiving things out of itself. "'Tis evident the mind knows not things immediately, but only by the intervention of the ideas it has of them" (IV., 4). His philosophy proceeds throughout on this principle. The object of the understanding when it thinks is an idea. The mind has intuitive knowledge, but it consists in the perception of the immediate agreement or disagreement of two ideas. Knowledge in general is the perception of the agreement or repugnance of ideas. Judging from these expressions it looks as if the mind, even in perceiving by reflection its own states, does so by the intervention of the ideas it has of them. I have difficulty in believing that he meant this, but his language carries this with it. We see how necessary it is, if we would get at the exact truth, to abandon the whole ideal theory of Locke and to return to the natural theory that we at once perceive things.

It appears to me that Locke very much identified ideas and things. He is not very well able to say how from ideas in the mind we reach things without the mind. The truth is, the question of the legitimacy or illegitimacy of arguing from things internal to things external was not expressly started at that time. He seems, at times at least, to proceed on the principle of causation; we have an idea in the mind and see that there is no cause within the mind and we argue a cause without the mind. But this proceeds on the necessary law of cause and effect, which is not justified by his experiential theory. It is supposed that we argue from an idea to an external object believed to be extended. But there is no extension in the idea, and we cannot logically argue from an unextended effect to an extended object, for this would place in the conclusion an entirely new object not in the premise. He regards the primary ideas of bodies as *resemblances* of the ideas, but how can he know that they are so unless he has known both and compared them? Altogether it is clear to me that Locke left this whole subject of the relation of the objective external state to the subjective idea in an uncertain state. Since his day it has passed through the idealism of Berkeley and the skepticism of Hume; Reid and Hamilton have sought to bring it back to a natural realism, while Kant, and of a later date Spencer, have introduced each of them new and important elements. We still need to have the subject cleared up; and this I am convinced will be done sooner or later, though it will be a difficult work. A statement with a critical examination of the opinions of the great thinkers now named, and a judicious criticism, may help to secure this end.

Meanwhile we have an important principle held by Locke, which has been overlooked by others, and which, as it appears to me, ought to be brought into prominence in the present state of the discussion. He has no very satisfactory way of reaching things, but when he reaches them he holds that our perceptions, our faculties generally, our intuitions, our reason, all look to things. Kant, in this respect, instead of advancing beyond Locke, has fallen behind him. The German philosopher did improve upon the English one when he showed that there were in the mind *a priori* principles anterior to experience. But then he made these, not perceptions of things, but forms imposed upon our perceptions of objects, adding to them and modifying them. In this respect he has been followed by Hamilton. It is time to repudiate this Kantian doctrine and return to the natural system which makes our primitive perceptions contemplate things. Locke meant to hold this system: " Had they examined the ways whereby men come to the knowledge of many universal truths they would have found them to result in the minds of men *from the being of things themselves* when duly considered " (I., 4).

SECTION XII.

GENERAL REVIEW OF LOCKE'S PHILOSOPHY.

I. We see what he denies: all innate ideas. Under this he asserts that there is nothing in the mind at its birth; it is a sheet of white paper. In attacking the views that were commonly entertained in his day he did philosophy much service. He was successful in showing that the

mind was not born with a set of ideas, in the sense of perceptions actually formed or ready to come forth on occasion.   He was evidently right in holding that the mind
has not an original repository of abstract and general notions, such as those of space, of time, of infinity, and moral
good.   He showed that all general notions and maxims
were formed out of particular instances by the exercise of
the faculties.

On the other hand he carried his negations too far.
Even a sheet of paper, though it has no characters, has
properties without which there could be no writing on it.
So it is with the mind; it has certain powers which are
native, which, indeed, might be called innate.   These
powers have rules and limits; they can do certain work;
in short, they are laws or principles.   A *tabula rasa*, or
blank paper, is not the fittest emblem of them.   Leibnitz
has a better.   It is not, he says, merely like bare marble;
it is like marble with veins in it, fitting it to become a
statue, say of Hercules.   It has "inclinations, dispositions,
habitudes, and natural virtualities" (*Nouv.-Ess.*, Pref.).
Locke, as we have seen, is obliged constantly to appeal to
judgments which the mind pronounces at once, and which
are necessary.   These show that there are innate regulating principles in the mind, supporting and guaranteeing
great truths.

II. Locke has two grand inlets of knowledge—sensation
and reflection.   But he has also faculties operating upon
these, such as perception, discernment, comparison, composition, abstraction.   These actually form our ideas.
Locke has not been able to state very clearly the relation
between these inlets and the faculties.   What, for instance,
is the difference between sensation as an inlet, and perception as directed to the ideas supposed to be introduced by
sensation?   Do they not, in fact, perform the same func-

tion, namely, give us a knowledge of bodily objects? It has been shown above that the faculties in their exercise give us new ideas, such as those of time and moral good, which cannot be had from either sensation or reflection, or from the two combined. It is clear that in a correct philosophy the inlets and the faculties should not be separated—they should be combined; and the faculties should be so unfolded and determined as to settle for us—what Locke was so anxious to do—the boundaries of our intellectual vision, and let every man " know the length of his tether."

III. No man has seen more clearly than Locke that our primitive perceptions are all individual. We perceive of these two straight lines that they cannot enclose a space; that the shortest distance between these two points is a straight line. Locke also sees that our general maxims are formed out of these particular instances, but he does not see precisely how this is done. In fact it is accomplished by the generalization of the singular exercises. We perceive of these two straight lines that they cannot enclose a space, and we discover that we would say the same of every other two lines, and so reach the general truth. Locke acknowledges that these generalized maxims serve some useful purposes, particularly in settling forever some disputed points. But he does not see how they accomplish such ends. It is because, when properly generalized, they are the expression of the constitutional principles of the mind, looking at things, and pronouncing a judgment as to what is involved in things.

IV. Locke had great difficulty in reaching realities. The mind perceived, and retained, and compared only ideas, and he had no legitimate way of arguing from these ideas in the mind any external things. His theory seemed to imply that the mind itself was only perceived by ideas coming in by reflection. But Locke was in fact a determined realist, believing in both mind and body, and that he knew things. Thus he made all our primitive perceptions, all our intuitions, our knowledge, and our common reason to look at things and all judgments to be pronounced about things.

NOTICE OF BERKELEY.

GEORGE BERKELEY was born March 12, 1685, in the vale of the Nore, near Thomastown, in County Kilkenny, in the south of Ireland. In 1700 he entered Trinity College, Dublin, where his favorite studies were mathematics and metaphysics. He began while there *A Commonplace Book*, in which we see as in a glass the rise and development of the new views which rose up in his mind. He became tutor in the family of Dr. William Molyneux, a great admirer of Locke, and was introduced to the *Essay on Human Understanding*, which had become famous. The other philosophical writers studied by him seem to have been Descartes, Hobbes, Malebranche, and he must have known the works of Peter Brown, Provost of Trinity College, and of King, Archbishop of Dublin. In 1709 he published his *Essay toward a new Theory of Vision*, in which he showed that the eye is not immediately percipient of distance. He afterward lived for some time in England, where he became acquainted with such men as Samuel Clarke, Addison, Steele, Swift, and Arbuthnot, and took a tour on the continent of Europe. He returned to Ireland in 1721, and became Dean of Derry in 1724. He was now seized with an impulse to set up a university in Bermuda to Christianize the Indians, and

persuaded the government to favor his scheme and a number of influential people to subscribe funds. In prosecu-
tion of this scheme he sailed for America, and landed at
Newport, in Rhode Island, in 1729. He lived for some
years in a house in the neighborhood still standing, and
was a favorite with those who came in contact with him ;
but not being able to carry out his Bermuda purpose he returned to his own country and was made Bishop of Cloyne.
At this period of his life he strongly recommended the virtues of tar-water, which he mixes up with his philosophic
theories. In his declining life he retired to Oxford and
became enamored with the Platonic philosophy, toward
which he had always been tending, even when he was under the influence of Locke. He died in 1753.

It is not very difficult to estimate the intellectual calibre
and the character of Berkeley. From an early date he
was addicted to dreamy reflection. "I was distrustful at
eight years old, and consequently by nature disposed for
these new doctrines." In gazing so intently into the
spiritual world the material covering was lost sight of.
He was possessed of great acuteness and ingenuity, but
was not distinguished for good sense or shrewdness. The
fact is, Berkeley was a visionary in everything. His Bermuda project and his belief in tar-water were not wilder
than his philosophy. It is amusing meanwhile to observe
how he claimed to be so practical. He convinced British
statesmen of great shrewdness, by an array of calculations,
that the best way of converting the Indians and of Chris-
tianizing the continent of America was by a college insti-
tuted at Bermuda. By an undiscerning agglomeration of
facts he convinced numbers in his own day, and he has
had believers in Ireland almost to our day, that tar-water
could cure all manner of diseases. In like way he persuaded himself that his philosophy is the expression of

vulgar belief and the perfection of common-sense. He
professes " to be eternally banishing metaphysics and recalling men to common-sense," ",to remove the mist and veil
of words," and to be " more for reality than other philosophers."

His style is acknowledged, on all hands, to be graceful
and attractive. He avoids, as Locke does, all scholastic and
technical phrases. As Locke affected the style of the
conversation which he had heard among the upper classes,
so Berkeley adopted the style of the literature of his day,
that is, of the wits of Queen Anne. This mode of composition has its disadvantages. If it has the ease of conversation and literature, it has also the looseness. Berkeley
confesses that he is by no means very precise in his use of
language : " Blame me not if I use my words sometimes
in some latitude ; this is what cannot be helped. It is
the fault of language that you cannot always apprehend
the clear and determinate meaning of my words." His
editor complains of "the chronic tendency to misconceive"
Berkeley's philosophy. His admirers are ever telling us
that he has been misunderstood, and in particular that his
opponents of the Scottish school, such as Baxter, Reid,
Beattie, and Stewart, do not apprehend his meaning. His
opponents are apt to feel, if not to say, that his speculations are so undefined that any one may form the shape
that suits him out of the cloud. Those attacking him.sup-
pose that he denies the existence of matter ; those defending him maintain that he holds resolutely by the existence
of matter. But surely there is some defect in a philosophic writer who has so expounded his doctrine that it
is forever misunderstood by able and candid minds. With
all these imperfections we feel that some of his works,
such, for instance, as *Three Dialogues between Phylas
and Philonous*, are the finest philosophic dialogues in the

English tongue, and are worthy of being placed alongside those of Plato.[1]

I am now to examine the chief points in his philosophy, so far as they relate to Locke, who preceded him, and to Hume, who professed to carry out his principles.

Theory of Vision.—Berkeley is best known in connection with this theory, which he expounded in his *Essay toward a New Theory of Vision* (1709) and defended in his *Theory of Vision Vindicated and Explained* (1733); and, indeed, in most of his works. Professor Fraser is of the opinion that in respect of his theory he has not so much originality as is commonly attributed to him. " He takes the invisibility of distance in the line of sight for granted as a common scientific truth of the time." It is well known that there were notices by Descartes of the way by which the eye perceives distances, and Malebranche specifies some of the signs by which distance is estimated. William Molyneux, in a treatise on optics, published in 1690, declared that distance of itself is not to be perceived, for " 'tis a line or a length presented to the eye with its end toward us, which must therefore be only a point and that is invisible " (I., 17); and then he shows that distance is chiefly perceived by means of interjacent objects, by the estimate we make of the comparative magnitude of bodies or their faint colors: this for objects considerably remote ; as to nigh objects their distance is perceived by the turn of the eyes or the angle of the optic axis. Locke, in the fourth edition of his Essay, mentions a problem put to him by Molyneux, whether, if a cube and a sphere were placed before a blind man who was made to see, he would be able

---

[1] The standard edition of Berkeley's works is *The Works of George Berkeley, D.D.*, 4 vols., by Professor Alexander Campbell Fraser. See, by the same author, *Selections from Berkeley* and *Berkeley*, in the " Philosophic Classics."

to tell which is the globe and which the cube, to which
both Molyneux and Locke answered " not." These statements by well-known philosophers were known to all in-
terested in such studies before Berkeley's work appeared.
But the *New Theory of Vision* treated of the subject
specially and in a more elaborate way, and has commonly
got the credit, not certainly of originating the doctrine,
but of establishing it.   Professor Fraser has shown that
Berkeley all along meant his views as to vision to establish
a far more important principle, that by all the senses we
perceive only signs of mental realities, a doctrine cherished
by him from an early date, but kept in the background in
his early work.

Idea.—Berkeley takes the word not in the sense of
Plato or the schoolmen, but in that of Descartes and Locke,
specially the latter.   The literal meaning always stuck to
it in Locke's apprehension, and breeds inextricable confusion.   He habitually regards the object of the mind when
it thinks as an idea in the sense of image.   He supposes
there is such an image when we use the senses, even such
senses as smelling and hearing, and he seeks for such an
image when we think of space, time, and eternity.   He
sees the difficulty in the mind forming an idea—in this
sense—of the product of abstraction and generalization.
He acknowledges that it doth " require some pains and
skill to form this general idea of a triangle," " for it must
be neither oblique nor rectangle, neither equilateral, equi-
crural, nor scalenum, but all and none of these at once.   In
effect it is somewhat imperfect that cannot exist ; an idea
wherein some parts of several different and inconsistent
ideas are put together."   Upon this Berkeley remarks :
" After reiterated efforts and pangs of thought to apprehend the general idea of a triangle, I have found it altogether incomprehensible " (I., 146).   " The idea of a man

that I frame to myself, must be either of a white, or a black, or a tawny, or a straight, or a crooked, a tall or a low, or a middle-sized man" (I., 142). Here, as in so many other cases, he has sharpness enough to detect the errors of the prevailing philosophy, but not clearness or comprehension enough to set it right. He would use the word as Locke had done: "I take the word idea for any of the immediate objects of sense or understanding" (I., 55). But then this object is an image: "By idea I mean any sensible or imaginable thing" (IV., 457). "Properly speaking it is the picture of the imagination's making. This is the likeness of and referred to the real idea or (if you will) thing" (445). He rejects, as I believe he ought, abstract ideas in the sense of Locke, that is, in the sense of images of qualities; and he claims it as his merit that he gets rid in this way of those grand abstractions, such as matter and substance, existence and extension, space and time, to which philosophers have given an independent being, and set up as rivals to Deity. But while he has exposed the errors of Locke, he has not established the positive truth. It turned out that David Hume, taking advantage of his doctrine, undermined, by a like process, the separate existence of personal identity and power, of mind and morality.

Abstract and General Ideas.—His defective views on this subject perplexes his whole philosophy. He takes credit for removing abstractions out of speculation that we may contemplate realities. And it is quite true that we cannot form an abstract idea in the sense of likeness or phantasm. We cannot form in the mind an image of whiteness as we do of a lily, of redness as we do of a rose, of humanity as we do of man. We have to bring in here the distinction known to Aristotle, between *phantasm* (image) and *noema* (notion). An abstract is not a *phan-*

tasm, an exercise of the mere reproductive, recalling or imaging power of the mind ; but a *notion*, the product of the elaborative or discursive—of the comparative powers, in fact—specially of the power which perceives the relation of part and whole, of an attribute to that concrete object of which it is an attribute.   Having seen a lily I can ever afterward image the lily—this is the phantasm of Aristotle.   But I can exercise another mental operation regarding it, and the product is the noema of Aristotle : I can consider its whiteness and not its shape or size, and when I do so I have an abstract notion about which I can pronounce judgments and reason.   On rare occasions Berkeley had a glimpse of what is involved in abstraction, as in his *Principles of Human Knowledge:* " And here it must be acknowledged that a man may consider a figure merely as triangular without attending to the particular qualities of the angles or relations of the sides.   So far he may abstract ; but this will never prove that he can frame an abstract general inconsistent idea [in the sense of image] of a triangle.   In like manner we may consider Peter so far forth as man, so far forth as animal, without framing the forementioned abstract idea [image], either of man or animal ; inasmuch as all that is perceived is not considered " (I., 148).   He says that " there is a great difference between considering length without breadth, and having an idea or of imagining length without breadth."   Speaking of the qualities abstracted he acknowledges that " it is not difficult to form general propositions and reasonings about these qualities without mentioning any other " (I., 284).   Had he taken as much pains in unfolding what is contained in " considering " a figure as triangular, and Peter as man, without considering other qualities and what is involved in " forming general propositions and reasonings about qualities," as he has taken to expel abstract ideas in the sense of phantasms, he would have saved his own philosophy, and philosophy generally from his day to this, from an immense conglomeration of confusion.

Much the same may be said of the General Idea, which Locke confounded with the Abstract Idea, under the phrase abstract general idea. These two evidently differ. An abstract notion is the notion of an attribute, a general notion is a notion of objects possessing a common attribute, or common attributes. We cannot form, in the sense of likeness, a general idea. An image, as Berkeley saw, must always be singular, whereas a general notion, the notion of a class, must embrace an indefinite number of individuals, all that possess the quality or qualities which bring the objects into a class. There can be no phantasm formed of the individuals in the class, which are innumerable, nor of the attributes, which are abstracts. At times he had a glimpse of what is implied in a general idea, but he does not pursue it, and he speedily loses sight of it. "Now, if we will annex a meaning to our words, and speak only of what we can conceive, I believe we shall acknowledge that an idea, which considered in itself is particular, becomes general by being made to represent or stand for all other particular ideas of the same sort "(I., 145). But what constitutes the *sort* and the same *sort ?* Had he proceeded to answer this question he might have found the exact truth. A sort is composed of things assorted, and assorted because possessing a quality or qualities in common, and must embrace all the objects possessing the quality or qualities. In looking at the things thus assorted, we see that the affirmations we make apply to all and each of the objects of the class, so that when a geometrician draws a black line of an inch in length, " this, which is in itself a particular line, is nevertheless, in regard to its signification, general, since, as it is there used, it represents all particular lines whatsoever, so that what is demonstrated of it is demonstrated of all lines, in other words, of a line in general" (*ib.*).   This is the general idea I stand up for, and I hold that it, and the abstract idea as above described, may be made the object of the understanding when it thinks, and that we can pronounce judgments upon it, and reason about it.   This is, in fact, what we do in mathematics and in all the sciences.

While he set himself in an indiscriminating manner against abstract general ideas, Berkeley was not, as he has been commonly represented, a nominalist.   His aim was to carry us away both from abstracts and names to individual things.   According to him "ideas become general by a particular idea standing for all the ideas of the sort," and so, "certainly it is not impossible but a man may arrive at the knowledge of all real truth as well without as with signs, had he a memory and imagination more strong and capacious," and therefore "reasoning and science doth not altogether depend on word or names'"(IV., 467).

Existence.—In every intelligent exercise we know ourselves as existing in a particular state, say thinking or willing.   Our knowledge of ourselves and the particular state, say thinking, are mixed up, but we can so separate them as to consider ourselves as existing.   This does not show that our existence depends on our perception.   We perceive ourselves to exist because we already exist.   So far as external objects are concerned, we perceive them by the eye as extended and colored, but we can, if we choose, consider them as existing apart from the color, apart even from our perception of them.   Of course our perception is implied in our perceiving them ; but this does not prove that our perception is necessary to their existence.   In fact we perceive them because they exist.   Unwilling to admit abstractions of any kind, Berkeley argued that the objects could not exist apart from the perception; hence his maxim, *esse est percipi*. I admit that a thing perceived must exist; but this does not imply, according to the rules of logic, the converse proposition, that a thing in order to exist must be perceived. I allow *percipi est esse*, but not *esse est percipi*. There were rocks deposited in our earth before there was a man to perceive them. We may believe that at this moment there are flowers in forests which have never been trod by human foot. The external thing, be it matter or be it idea, must exist in order to my perceiving it—it is *esse* before it is *percipi*.

But then he explains that he does not mean that in order to the existence of a thing it must be perceived by the individual, it may be perceived by other finite beings, it must be perceived by God. But this admission implies that in order to its existence it is not necessary that we should perceive it; in other words, the thing may exist independent of our perception of it. "I will grant you that extension, color, etc., may be said to be without the mind in a double respect; that is, independent of our will and distinct from the mind " (IV., 667). And if it exist independent of our perception it may exist independent of the perception of other created beings. There is nothing, then, in the nature of our perception, considered in itself, implying that the existence of the object implies perception. Berkeley speaks as if the existence of a thing independent of mind is meaningless and contradictory; is repugnant, as he expresses it. But surely I can conceive of a thing as existing out of and independent of the mind perceiving it, and if there be evidence I can believe it to exist. True, if I believe it to exist on reasonable ground, I must have perceived it myself, or have the testimony of some one who has perceived it. But then I can conceive it to exist whether I have perceived it or no; whether, in-

deed, I believe in its existence or no. In all this there is
nothing self-repugnant. "But, then, to a Christian, it
cannot surely be shocking to say that the real tree existing
without his mind is truly known and comprehended by
(that it exists in) the infinite mind of God" (I., 330).
That everything is known to God and comprehended by
his infinite mind will be admitted by all Christians, by all
who believe in an omnicient God. But, then, this does
not follow from the nature of perception, but from our
belief derived otherwise of the guardian care of God, a
belief most readily obtained when we acknowledge the
reality of external objects. Observe how dextrously he
slides from one meaning of comprehension, from the
meaning "embraced in the understanding," to "exist in,"
which is an entirely different thing. I comprehend the
deed of a son murdering his father, but this does not make
the deed exist in me. Not only so, but I hold it to be in
every way most reverent, not to speak of that deed of
murder as existing in the mind of the good God. Berkeley
often writes as if it were not possible for God to make a
thing, having an existence out of himself, with any power
in itself. This, surely, is a limitation of the divine power
by no means very reverential. Believing the plunging of
the knife into the bosom of the murdered man to exist out
of me, I believe it to be most becoming to represent it as
also existing out of God.

He is greatly alarmed for the consequences which might
follow, provided it is admitted that there can be existence
independent of perception. "Opinion that existence was
distinct from perception of horrible consequence. It is
the foundation of Hobbes' doctrine" (IV., 459). But fact
and truth never lead to evil consequences, which errors,
even well-meant errors, commonly do. The good bishop
never dreamed that his favorite principle would furnish a

starting-point to Hume. I have noticed passages in Berkeley which look as if they might have suggested the basis of Hume's skeptical theory. Hume opens his *Treatise of Human Nature:* "All the perceptions of the human mind resolve themselves into two distinct kinds, which I call *impressions* and *ideas.* The difference betwixt these consists in the degrees of force and liveliness with which they strike upon the mind and make their way into our thought or consciousness. Those perceptions which enter with most force and violence we may name *impressions;* and under this name I comprehend all our sensations, passions, and convictions as they make their first appearance in the soul. By *ideas,* I mean the faint images of these in thinking and reasoning." Might not the whole doctrine, and the language employed, and the distinction drawn, have risen up in his shrewd, unsatisfied mind as he read at the close of a long discussion in the *Principles:* "What do we perceive besides our ideas and sensations?" (I., 157). He specifies the very distinction between the two, the one more lively, the other more faint. "The ideas of sense are more strong, lively, and distinct than those of imagination" (170). "The ideas imprinted in the senses by the author of nature are called real things, and those excited in the imagination being less regular, vivid, and constant are more commonly termed ideas" (172). Hume thus got his very phraseology, *impressions* (from *imprinted*) and *ideas,* and the distinction between the two, as lying in the difference of force or strength, liveliness or distinctness. Hume accepted the bishop's doctrine and drove it logically to a conclusion which did not admit of an argument for the existence of a God to uphold these impressions or sensations and ideas.

Matter.—The whole philosophy of Locke proceeds on the supposition that we perceive only ideas. His theory

of knowledge is a movement in a circle. An idea is the
object we perceive ; the object we perceive is an idea.
This idea was regarded by him as an image of an object
out of the mind which it resembles and represents. But
it was perceived at an early date that he had and could
have no proof of this, indeed no proof of the existence
of matter. Man can take no immediate cognizance of
matter ; and logic will not allow us from a mere idea in
the mind to argue the existence of something beyond the
mind. This was the condition of speculative philosophy
in Great Britain when Berkeley thought out his ingenious
theory. He saw it to be very unsatisfactory, if the mind
can perceive nothing but the idea, to argue that there must
be a material object of which it is a copy. So he boldly
declared we are not required to believe in anything but
the idea. All that we perceive is the idea. We have no
proof of the existence of anything else. If there be anything else it must be unknown. Every purpose that could
be served by this supposed external thing may be accomplished by the idea. "If, therefore, it were possible for
bodies to exist without the mind, yet to hold they do so
must be a very precarious opinion, since it is to suppose,
without any reason at all, that God has created innumerable beings that are utterly useless and serve no manner
of purpose. In short, if there were external bodies, it is
impossible we should ever come to know it; and, if it were
not, we might have the very same reason to think that
there were that we have now" (I., 165). Berkeley thus
started what Hamilton would call a presentation theory of
sense-perception ; that is, that the mind looked directly on
the object, the object with him, however, being the idea
with nothing beyond. Reid followed : discovering that
Locke could never reach the existence of matter by a process of reasoning, he insisted that the existence of matter

was suggested by instinct, intuition, or common-sense, there being first a sensation, this instinctively raising a perception of an external thing. Hamilton took a bolder and a more direct course than Reid : discarding, as Reid had done, the idea of Locke and of Berkeley; and discarding, too, the *suggestion* of Reid, he asserted that we look directly on matter, are immediately conscious of matter. Hamilton, like Berkeley, is a presentationist; but Berkeley says that the object before the mind is an idea, whereas Hamilton says it is a material object possessing extension.

At this point it is of all things the most important to determine in what sense Berkeley admits, and in what sense he denies, the existence of matter. He is ever asserting, and asserting in strong language, that he believes in the existence of bodies. Yet he speaks constantly of his aim being to expel matter from the universe: " Were it necessary to add any further proof against the existence of matter " (I., 16 and *passim*). But he is a firm upholder of the existence, not of abstract matter, but of individual bodies : " I do not argue against the existence of any one thing that we can apprehend, either by sense or reflection. That the things I see with my eyes and touch with my hands do exist, really exist, I make not the least question. The only thing whose existence we do deny is that which philosophers call matter or corporeal substance." In the interests of religion he is tremulously afraid of allowing the existence of matter as a substance. " Matter once allowed, I defy any man to prove that God is not matter" (IV., 442) ; as if matter did not, like mind, supply evidence of the existence of its maker and disposer. He is for expelling the substance, matter, to which some were attributing an existence independent of God; but infidels in our day are quite ready to make a like use of matter con-

sidered as a mere phenomenon : they argue that it does
not need a God to support it. He is right, so I think, in
maintaining that in regard to body we should not be required to believe in more than we can perceive by the
senses, more than we see, and feel, and taste, and smell,
and hear. But then we perceive by the senses much more
than he is disposed to allow. He means by idea " any
sensible or imaginable thing." An idea must be in the
mind, so he argues that the whole, perception and thing
perceived, must be in the mind. _ " The tree or house,
therefore, which you think of is conceived by you."
"What is conceived is surely in the mind " (I., 291, 292).
"Nothing properly but persons, *i.e.*, conscious things, do
exist. All other things are not so much existences, as
manners of the existence of persons ; " on which Professor Fraser asks, " Is an extended thing a mode in which
a person exists ? " (IV., 469). He showed in his *New
Theory of Vision* that color is in the mind, and then, in
his *Principles* and later works, that extension, as an idea,
must also be in the mind. Professor Fraser thus expounds
him, I believe fairly : "When we do our utmost by imagination to conceive bodies existing externally or absolutely,
we are, in the very act of doing so, making them ideas,
not of sense indeed, but of imagination. The supposition
itself of their individual existence, makes them ideas, inasmuch as it makes them imaginary objects, dependent on
an imagining mind " (I., 123). Still he stands up for the
reality of body : " The table I write on I say exists, that I
see and feel it, and if it were out of my study I should say
it existed, meaning thereby, that if I was in my study I
might perceive it, or that some other spirit does actually
perceive it" (I., 157). This is the very theory which,
passing through Hume and James Mill, has been elabo-
rated by John Stuart Mill into the doctrine of matter

being the "possibility of sensations." Every man of ordinary sense on first hearing this doctrine will be inclined to say, there must surely be some mistake, some confusion here, and this whether he is able to point it out or not. The misconceptions, I believe, are to be rectified by an inductive inquiry into what the senses really reveal. Looking simply to the testimony of our senses they make known something out of us and independent of us. In particular we know body as extended, we see it as extended in two dimensions, we feel it as with three dimensions. No doubt there is perception in all this, but perception is not extended in any sense, in one, two, or three dimensions. We perceive it as something different from our perception, and we perceive it as having something not in our perception, we perceive it, in short, as extended. This is an intuition carrying within itself its own evidence. As being self-evident it can stand the test of contradiction : we cannot believe the opposite ; we cannot be made to believe that the table before me has not length and breadth. It is also catholic or universal, as being in all men. Just as by the internal sense we know mind, so by the external senses we know matter. The evidence for the existence of the one is much the same as the evidence for the existence of the other. We cannot allow the one to set aside the other. We must accept both, and I defy any one to show that there is any repugnancy between them.

Extension perceived by Sight and Touch.—He puzzles himself and puzzles his editor greatly by his favorite maxim, that we do not see the same extension by the eye and by the touch. "The objects of sight and touch are two distinct things" (I., 56). Professor Fraser seems to go further, "colored extension is antithetical to felt extension." The perplexity arises from not observing precisely what we do perceive by means of these two senses. By the eye we do not perceive abstract extension, but an extended thing. It is the same with touch, we do not perceive mere extension, we perceive an extended thing. By a subsequent act of comparison, we may discover the two, the extended table seen and touched, to be the same thing. Surely there is no antithesis here, any more than there is between seeing first one side of a building, and then another side, between seeing the one side of a shield red, and the other black. By each of the senses we get a certain amount of information, which we combine in the one thing, which we discover to have extension, discovered both by the eye and by touch. Certainly the knowledge given by the touch in our ordinary apprehension of sensible objects mingles with that given by the eye, and indeed with that given by all the senses, and we superadd to all these the inferences which we have drawn. To intuitive perception by the eye a mountain is but a colored surface with a definite outline; but we combine in it all that we have known about mountains by touch and a gathered experience, that green is grass, that other green is a tree, that brown is a scar, and that sharp outline a precipice. There is no contradiction in all this.

Substance.—It is not to be wondered at that Berkeley should have been dissatisfied with Locke's doctrine on this subject. Locke denies very strongly and emphatically that he sets aside substance, and he is very angry at his opponent, Stillingfleet, when he says that he does so. He believes in substance; but then it can be made known neither by sensation nor reflection, and so it comes in very awkwardly in a system which acknowledges no other inlets of knowledge than these two. It is the unknown substratum or support of what is known. Berkeley did great service to philosophy by removing these crutches supposed to help, but really hindering, our conviction as to the reality of things. "Say you there might be a thinking substance—something unknown which perceives and supports and ties together the ideas. Say, make it appear that there is need of it, and you shall have it for me; I care not to take away anything I can see the least reason to think should exist" (IV., 443). I have always regretted that Reid and the Scottish school, in discarding the "idea" of Locke as coming between the thing perceived and perception, did not also abandon the "substance" of Locke as being equally useless and cumbersome. Berkeley seems to me to be farther and pre-eminently right when he maintains, in regard to matter, that we are to believe only in what is made known by the senses. "That the things I see with my eyes and touch with my hands do exist, really exist, I make not the least question. The only thing whose existence we deny is that which philosophers call matter or corporeal substance. And in doing of this there is no damage to the rest of mankind, who, I dare say, will never miss it. The atheist, indeed, will want the color of an empty name to support his impiety; and the philosophers may possibly find that they have lost a great handle for trifling and disputation" (I., 173). I am glad to find him saying farther, as if he had a reference to a mode of speaking in our day: "The philosophers talk much of a distinction betwixt absolute and relative things, considered in their own nature, and the same things considered with respect to us. I know not what they mean by 'things considered in themselves.' This is nonsense, jargon." I have, however, endeavored to show that Berkeley did not discover all that is involved in perception by the senses.

But is Matter a Substance? The answer to this question must depend on the definition which we give of substance. There is a sense, and this I believe the proper sense, in which both mind and matter are substances. It can be shown of both that they exist. It can be shown, secondly, of both, of matter as well as mind, that they are not created by our perceiving them. We perceive matter because it already exists. It exists whether we perceive it or no. It does not cease to exist because we have ceased to look at it. In this sense it has an independence, not, it may be, of God, but an independence of the percipient mind, of our perception of it. I am prepared to maintain that matter, like mind, has power of some kind. I do not assert that it has power independent of God— this is a question which carries us into a much higher region than our primitive perceptions. What I affirm is, that it has potency, influence of some kind. Now combine these three things: being, independence of our perceptions, and potency, and we have the true idea of substance. Thus understood, substance has no need of a substratum or support. Under God, who may himself be understood as a substance, it is its own support; and any other support would be a weakness. Everything possessing these three things may be regarded as a substance. Mind is a substance, for it has being, independence, and power. But matter is also a substance for the very same reasons.

Power.—His views on this subject are vague and unsatisfactory. He seems to regard all power as in God. He leaves no power whatever in body. "Matter neither acts, nor perceives, nor is it perceived." The first question here is: Is it true? Can we prove it? I believe we know things in this world, we know ourselves as having power, and bodies as having power upon each other. I believe them to have such power in our primitive cognition of them. Experience confirms this. According to Berkeley there is no relationship between material things, except that of coexistence and succession : one thing is a mere sign of another, and an arbitrary sign. These ideas which constitute all we perceive, can have no influence on each other. Now it seems to me that we are led to believe that they do act on each other. It can be shown that in all bodily actions there are two or more agents. A hammer strikes a stone and breaks it : the cause consists of the hammer and stone each in a certain state ; the effect consists of the same hammer and stone in another state, the hammer having lost the momentum which it had when it came in contact with the stone, and the stone being broken. It seems plain to me that the cause here is not a mere arbitrary sign of the effect ; the effect is the result of powers or properties of the agent. A second question may arise : What is the religious bearing of such a doctrine ? According to it God " useth no tool or instrument at all " (I., 312) ; there are no second causes in nature, but only natural signs. There is " no sharing betwixt God and nature or second causes in my doctrine." Is there not a risk that this very pious doctrine land us in the very impious conclusion, that if all action is of God, sinful action must also be of him ? If we have no knowledge of power in nature or in created mind, have we any proof of the existence of power in God ? The doctrine was eagerly seized by Hume, who showed that according to it the mind could form no idea of power beyond a custom of expecting that things which have been unvariably together in our experience will continue to be together. Left without the idea of power in the cognition of ourselves or earthly objects, we have really no ground except this same custom, carried illegitimately beyond our experience, (which can give us no knowledge of world-making) for arguing the existence of God from his works in nature.

Signs.—The great truth which Berkeley helped to

establish, that distance can be known by the eye only by means of signs supplied by touch, opened new views, which he carried out further than he was logically entitled. From the beginning he meant to use the theory of vision, to establish his favorite principle that we do not perceive extended things out of the perceiving mind: we perceive merely the signs of things. What the eye discerns is merely the sign of something else discovered by touch. "We see distances as we see shame or anger in the looks of a friend" (I., 63). In his later works he carries out the same principle to touch, and shows that it makes known simply heaven-appointed and heaven-organized symbols of reality beyond. But this view involves a mistake in starting, and a want of logic in the process. It is not correct to say that the eye does not immediately discover extended body; it looks directly on an extended colored surface. The eye may need the aid of the muscular sense to reveal space in three dimensions, but it at once perceives space in two dimensions; and we are thus put in a position to understand the farther information conveyed by touch. Our secondary knowledge implies primary knowledge, and the elements of the secondary knowledge must be found in the primary. If there be the idea of extension in the derived knowledge, there must have been the idea of extension in the original knowledge. The looks of a man reveal shame and anger, because we already know these by self-consciousness. Signs cannot reveal to us anything not otherwise known in its materials. We certainly have the idea of an extended thing, and this could never be made known to us by a sign which was not itself extended. Signs are merely the antecedents or concomitants of things which we are enabled to conceive because we know them otherwise. Little did Berkeley see in arguing that we only see signs of things, that he was preparing the way for the avenging skeptic, who allows the existence of the signs, but argues with David Hume and Herbert Spencer that the things signified are unknown and unknowable.

Lofty minds are apt to be particularly fascinated with the doctrine that nature is a system of universal symbolism. I believe as firmly as Berkeley ever did, that it is so; I believe with him that "the methods of nature are the language of its author" (I., 211). But I do so because the signs are real things, signs of other things. If the glass is visionary the things seen through it will be apt to be regarded as also visionary. As he advanced in life and enjoyed leisure in the bishopric of Cloyne, he eagerly turned to the study of Plato and the Neo-Platonists, and embodied the results in his *Siris, a Chain of Philosophical Reflections and Inquiries concerning the Virtues of Tar - Water.*

Mind.—Our author is very valiant in making inroads into the territories of his enemies; but meanwhile he leaves his own domain defenceless. "There is not any other substance than spirit, or that which perceives." But it is very difficult to tell us what he makes of spirit. Professor Fraser acknowledges, "Berkeley has no clear teaching about finite minds—*egos* as distinguished from the *Ego*" (IV., 638). Berkeley tells us, "the very existence of ideas constitutes the soul." "Consult, ransack the understanding; what find you there besides several perceptions or thoughts? Mind is a congeries of perceptions. Take away perceptions and you take away the mind. Put the perceptions and you put the mind" (IV., 438). Every one acquainted with the history of philosophy will perceive that this, the doctrine with which the young Berkeley started, is the very doctrine which Hume reaches: "Certainly the mind always and constantly thinks, and

we know this too. In sleep and trances the mind exists
not, there is no time, no succession of ideas" (IV.,
444).   No wonder the editor says, " As to personal identity
he is obscure."   I would rather say, he is clearly wrong.
He tells us again and again that mind or spirit is "not
knowable, not being an idea" (IV., 462); a doctrine far
lower than that of Locke, who maintains that we have an
idea of mind by means of Reflection.   " I have no idea of
a volition or act of the mind; neither has any other intelligence, for that were a contradiction " (IV., 446).   He
seeks to save himself from palpably absurd consequences
by drawing, in the second edition of his *Principles of
Human Knowledge*, the distinction between Idea and
Notion (taking the phrase, I believe, from Bishop Browne):
" It must be admitted, at the same time, that we have
some notion of soul or spirit, and the operations of the
mind, such as willing, loving, hating, inasmuch as we
know or understand the meaning of these words " (I., 170).
But he never accurately defined what he meant by Notion;
and his whole philosophy is left, in consequence, in an unsatisfactory condition.

In digging away the ground on which error has rested,
I do not believe that Berkeley has left to himself a foundation on which to build a solid philosophy. "I approve,"
he says, " of this axiom of the schoolmen, *Nihil est in in-
tellectu quod non prius fuit in sensu.* I wish they had
stuck to it. It had never taught them the doctrine of abstract ideas " (IV., 457). His editor is evidently staggered
with " this remarkable statement," and does not know
very well what to make of it. His doctrine on this subject is a great deal lower than that of Locke, who made
reflection as well as sensation an inlet of ideas, such as
those of time, and power, and spirit, by which he so far
counteracted the sensational tendency of his philosophy.

Berkeley is often appealing to intuition and reason in up-
holding his own favorite maxims, such as that there cannot be matter without mind, but has left no explanation
of the nature and laws of these ultimate principles, or defence of their legitimacy. His negative appeal is to some
"repugnancy," he does not tell us to what. These defects
in the foundation are not to be repaired by abutments in
the superstructure. There is a like defect in his ethical
principles: "Sensual pleasure is the *summum bonum.*
This is the great principle of morality. This once rightly
understood, all the doctrines, even the severest of the
gospels, may clearly be demonstrated. Sensual pleasure,
quâ pleasure, is good and desirable by a wise man. But
if it be contemptible 'tis not *quâ* pleasure but *quâ* pain;
or (which is the same thing) of loss of greater pleasure "
(IV., 457). This is a vastly more degraded view than that
taken by Shaftesbury, of whom he speaks so disparagingly.
We see how much need there was in that age of a Butler
to give a deeper foundation to morality than Locke or
Berkeley had done. There is greater need of a Butler
than of a Berkeley in our time.

His view of space and time is thus rendered by his
editor: "Finite Space is, with him, experience in unre-
sisted organic movement which is capable of being symbol-
ized in the visual consciousness of coexisting colors. Finite
Time is the apprehension of changes in our ideas, length
of time being measured by the number of changes. Infinite Space and Infinite Time, because inapprehensible by
intelligence, are dismissed from philosophy as terms void
of meaning, or which involve contradictions " (I., 117). If
our natural judgments were not meant to deceive us there
must be vastly more than this in Time, Space, and Infinity,
say, the Infinity of God.

There is a very general impression that the philosophy of Berkeley is favorable to religion. That he meant it to be so is certain; that many have felt it to be so should not be denied. Taken apart from his speculations about tar-water and the non-existence of matter, the general influ-ence of his writings is inspiring and ennobling, carrying us above the damp earth into the empyrean, where we breathe a pure and delicious atmosphere. His *Minute Philosopher* is distinguished by great acuteness, a lofty tone, and an alluring charm of manner and of style. The speakers appointed to oppose religion do not argue so searchingly as the objecting interlocutors do in Plato's dialogues; but they bring forward the current objections of the age, and the answer to them is complete. But our present inquiry is, What is the tendency of his system? And, whatever may be the immediate impression produced by it, the influence of a philosophy is determined by its logical consequences, which will come to be wrought out by some one. Hume declares that most of Berkeley's writings "form the best lessons of skepticism which are to be found either among the ancient or modern philoso-phers—Bayle not excepted," and he gives the reason, "they admit of no answer and produce no conviction." Hume certainly labored with all his might (and he was a mighty man) to make Berkeley teach lessons of skepticism. If bodies have an existence merely as perceived, people will argue that it may be the same with spirits; and Berkeley virtually allows the consequence. If matter has no substantial existence, why may it not be the same with mind? And, if so, what remains but Hume's sensations and ideas? Berkeley imagined he was getting new and special proof of the Divine existence by his doctrine of signs; but Hume came after him and showed that the signs suggested things beyond them merely by the association of ideas; merely by a phenomenon of sight suggesting a phenomenon of touch; in fact merely by the two having been together. In particular, he showed that two sensations, with an interval between, gendered the illusive feeling of the continued existence of the sentient agent.

PHILOSOPHIC SERIES.

CRITICAL NOTICES.

"Three eminently cogent and instructive pamphlets designed for exposition and defense of fundamental truths. The distinct but correlated subjects are treated with equal simplicity and power, and cover in brief much of the ground occupied by larger publications, together with much on independent lines of thought that lie outside their plan."—*Harper's Magazine.*

"It is a familiar experience, that there is a gain in clearness and condensation when one writes anew on subjects which one has previously handled in more copious treatises. In truth, an author himself often feels, when he has finished a book, that he is just prepared to write it. The effect of the discussion is to reduce his own thought to its lowest terms, and to disentangle it from surplus and irrelevant matter. The readers of Dr. McCosh's pamphlets will in this way reap the benefit of the author's earlier and more elaborate consideration of the same topics. An adherent, though not a servile adherent, of the Scottish school, he has brought to his inquiries for many years the best powers of a clear and vigorous intellect and of a mind well-informed in the history of speculation. * * * The titles of the numbers of "The Philosophic Series," which are yet to appear, indicate that they will deal with the most interesting and momentous questions which are now agitated among metaphysicians and speculative naturalists. It is gratifying to see that the venerable President of Nassau Hall retains all the freshness of his youthful interest in these grave problems, and is disposed to present in a form so convenient to readers the fruit of his ripened powers and of the mature studies of a life which has been largely devoted, and with distinguished success, to philosophical reflection."—*New York Tribune.*

"It is not unlikely to prove true in the end that the most useful, popular service which Dr. McCosh has rendered to the cause of right thinking and to sound philosophy of life, is his philosophic series, the first number of which, *Criteria of Diverse kinds of Truth, as opposed to Agnosticism. Being a treatise on Applied Logic,* we have perused with great satisfaction. Dr. McCosh has prepared in the compass of this little brochure of sixty 12 mo. pages, which can easily be read in a few hours, a treatise of the basis of knowledge and the method of reaching it, in doing this he has placed in front of the most influencial heresies of our times a luminous exposition of a sounder philosophy. * * * Brief as the treatise is it contains the mature conclusions of one of the foremost philosophers of the day and the outlines of consistent philosophy of life. The manual is written with directness and vigor and goes straight to the point of greatest need in the present condition of opinion."—*N. Y. Independent.*

"Dr. McCosh's work grows more interesting as he proceeds. There is something absolutely new in his treatment of the principle of causation. He shows that there is a duality or plurality in causation, also a duality or plur-

ality in the effect. The use of this fact is seen in the author's attempt to ad-
just the old doctrine of causation to the lately discovered doctrine of the con-
servation of energy or the persistence of force. * * * Dr. McCosh's
style is clear, bold and fervid, often rising into eloquence. He is easily
understood. For young men who wish to become acquainted with correct methods of testing the truth, nothing could be better than this series.
For busy men, also, this bird's-eye view of what the author calls 'a sober
philosophy,' will be found invaluable. 'He who runs may read.'"—*Columbus
Gazette.*

"This is the first of a promised series of pamphlets on some of the important subjects of modern philosophy. It need hardly be said that whatever
comes from Dr. McCosh's pen is characterized by remarkable vigor and clearness and even if the tone be somewhat dogmatic, it must be remembered
that it is the dogmatic tone of one of the ablest living leaders of Scotch
thought. The first of the series just referred to goes over partly the ground
of *Institutions* and the *Logic* of the same author. There has been much condensation and there are some valuable additions. The work has been prepared with special reference to the Agnosticism of the day, it is suf-
controversial to make it of interest to the general reader, it is suf-
simple to make it of value as an academic text-book of reference."—*Presby-
terian Review.*

"This first issue deals, in a masterly way, with the very popular but sui-
cidal error of agnosticism. It sets forth the criteria of first principles, the axioms of reasoning, and also those of individual facts, and their laws, and thus
teaches how to distinguish between different kinds of truth. It is thorough
and clear, and will be very helpful to those who have become unsettled either
by the opposing theories of scholars, or by the difficulties which surround almost every science when investigation is carried beyond the limit of the
knowable. The distinction here pointed out between necessary and probable
truths is of great importance. The want of this discrimination lies at the root
of the whole system of agnosticism ; and, we may add, of the religious dog-
matism which has characterized the later theology of Rome."—*The Church-
man.*

"Dr. McCosh's Philosophic Series will be likely to do great service among
thinking people. His views are sharply defined and in these papers briefly
expressed. No. III, on Developement will perhaps, receive the most general
attention, and it is worthy of it, both from what it recognizes as true in the
doctrine and what it rejects as false in the hasty inferences of some apostles of
that doctrine."

"Its style is so clear and direct, its presentation of the whole subject is so
natural and forcible, that many persons who habitually ignore discussions of
abstract topics, would be charmed into a new intellectual interest by giving
Dr. McCosh's work a careful consideration."—*N. Y. Observer.*

"This is not a controversial dissertation, but a clear and profound statement of the facts, and laws of intellectual and moral being as they bear
directly on the question of spiritual knowledge, or the basis of faith. Dr.
McCosh has the happy faculty of stating profound and abtruse reasonings and
conclusions, with such clearness and felicity that the intellectual reader has no
difficulty in following his thought and understanding the points he makes."—
N. Y. Evangelist.